100 AUTHORS
WHO SHAPED WORLD HISTORY

Christine N. Perkins

A Bluewood Book

Published in 1996 by
Bluewood Books
A Division of The Siyeh Group, Inc.,
P.O. Box 689
San Mateo, CA 94401

ISBN 0-912517-21-2

Printed in the USA

Designed by Bill Yenne
with the help of Azia Yenne

Proofread by Joan Hayes

Edited by Barbara Krystal

Key to front cover illustration: The main picture is Samuel Clemens (Mark Twain). Clockwise from Clemens are: Louisa May Alcott, Rudyard Kipling, Charles Dickens, Toni Morrison, Michael Crichton and Amy Tan.

The illustrations in this book are by Tony Chikes, with the following exceptions:
AGS Archives: 6, 7, 9, 19, 20, 23, 24, 27, 28, 32, 34, 37, 40-42, 51, 53, 55, 59, 61
© Jerry Bauer, courtesy of Farrar, Strauss & Giroux
© Mary Cross, courtesy of Dutton/Plume Publicity: 99
John Earle, courtesy of G.P. Putnam's Sons: 107
Marion Ettlinger, courtesy of Ballantine Books: 104
Jonathan Exley, courtesy of Ballantine Books: 103
Paul Farber, courtesy of Dramatists Play Service: 86
Farrar, Strauss & Giroux: 94
© Robert Foothorap, courtesy of G.P. Putnam's Sons: 109
© Gentil & Heyers, courtesy of Farrar, Strauss & Giroux: 91
© Kate Kunz, courtesy of Farrar, Strauss & Giroux: 96
© Chris Peterson: 43, 56, 64, 65
© Joyce Ravid, courtesy of Ballantine Books: 100
Jerry Samuelson, courtesy of G.P. Putnam's Sons: 97
Vadim Vahrameev 77
© Bill Yenne 63

TABLE OF CONTENTS

46.-47.
23.-26.   41.-45.
             38.-40.
          27.-37.

16. 18. 20.
17. 19. 21.
        22.

1. 2. 3. 4. 5. 6. 7. 8. 9. 10. 11. 12. 13. 14. 15.

850 BC   1000 AD   1850

49.
53.-56.   61.-63.   69.-71.   78.-80.   87.-88.   98.-99.
48. 50. 51. 52.   57.-60.   66.-68.   75.-77.   86.   92.-97.
        64.-65.   72.-74.   81.   82. 83.-85.   89.-91.   100.

1850   1953

INTRODUCTION

The greatest treasure of the human race is its literature. It defines the very soul and spirit of humanity. The stories of Homer and the morals of Aesop are as alive today as they were in the ninth and sixth centuries BC.

In the Renaissance, literature was linked to humanism, the ideals of scholarship, and the art of the use of language. For many centuries, the author was the observer and commentator. In the Age of Enlightenment, which occurred in Europe in the eighteenth century, the author emerged as a sort of spiritual leader through whom great ideas developed and were commented upon.

Literature delights us in our pursuit of happiness and provides us with the metaphors that enliven our language.

The works of William Shakespeare remind us of this, and certainly Shakespeare reminds us of how great literature survives the test of time.

Since Shakespeare's time, authors have been seen as either trusted guardians of cultural ideals or creators of popular entertainment. In some cases, the author became both. In the nineteenth century, William Makepeace Thackery and Alfred Tennyson characterized the former, while Samuel "Mark Twain" Clemens and Charles Dickens characterized the latter. However, today we rank Clemens' *Adventures of Tom Sawyer*, and many of Dickens' works at the apogee of literary masterpieces. Certainly Herman Melville was regarded as a popular writer, yet *Moby Dick* is among the most important works of philosophical fiction.

In the twentieth century, authors have become super-stars. Authors such as, but certainly not limited to, James Michener and Stephen King, sell millions of books, Anne Rice and Amy Tan have developed strong followings that eagerly await their every novel, and authors such as Michael Crichton are being offered million-dollar movie contracts.

The selection of writers for this volume was a daunting task, for indeed every author herein included reminds us of another author of equal stature who could easily have been included.

In the selection process, we endeavored to achieve both historical and stylistic balance. We could easily have selected 100 great authors from each of the past three centuries. We could have focussed entirely on popular writers or so-called "serious" writers, but to include Edgar Rice Burroughs along with Edna St. Vincent Millay is an illustrative celebration of the great richness and diversity of our literary heritage.

Laura Ingalls Wilder and D.H. Lawrence could not be more different in style and substance, yet it would not have been possible to omit either from this survey. All were, and are, important and each has an audience which is important to any overall consideration of literary history.

This book is a collection of brief biographies of a mere handful of the great authors who have shaped history. We hope that it will be found to be representative of a cross section of great authors. Beyond this, it is a celebration of our entire literary heritage.

HOMER
850-? BC

It has been said that of **Homer**'s life, the ancients told much but knew little. He was probably a blind poet, wandering from city to city, making a living by reciting his poetry. The uncertainty about his life is summed up in the couplet: "Seven Grecian cities claimed great Homer dead, Through which the living Homer begged his bread."

It is probable that Homer was associated with the court of some ruler, like the bard Phemius in Homer's *Odyssey*.

Epic poetry certainly arose among the Greeks on the western coast of Asia Minor. Various facts point to the period between 850 and 800 BC as the time when Homer wrote the *Iliad* and the *Odyssey*, his two great epics. The *Iliad,* the older of the two, narrates an episode of the Trojan War. **Achilles**, a Greek chieftain, quarrels with Agamemnon, the commander in chief, over the possession of a captured slave girl.

Achilles refuses to fight against the Trojans, and in his absence the Greeks are defeated. To avert an utter rout, Achilles allows his friend Patroclus to enter the battle. Patroclus is killed by Hector, the Trojan leader. Achilles, forgetting his quarrel in the desire for revenge, re-enters the war and slays Hector.

The *Odyssey* tells of the wanderings of Odysseus, one of the leaders of the Greek expedition against Troy.

For ten years he wanders in a series of marvelous adventures meeting giants, enchantresses, and devouring monsters. Having lost all his men in these escapades, he arrives safely in his native Ithaca.

Here Odysseus finds his wife Penelope, beset by many suitors, who suppose that he is dead. With the help of his son Telemachus and a few trusty servants, he kills the suitors and reestablishes himself in his kingdom.

Other poems which bear the name of Homer, were executed by later poets. These are the Homeric Hymns, short narratives of the adventures of the gods, and a mock epic, *The Battle of the Frogs and Mice.*

Homer.

Ancient mythical stories portrayed this liberated slave from Phyrygia as a wise, humpbacked buffoon who associated with such famed contemporaries as King Croesus of Lydia, the courtesan Rhodopis, Solon the Athenian lawgiver, and the Seven Wise Men. **Aesop** is reputed to have died at the hands of the citizens of Delphi, who were insulted when he said that their celebrated oracle enabled them to profit from mankind's misfortunes. The Delphians vindictively planted a sacred golden bowl in his luggage, judged him a thief, and threw him from a cliff.

For generations, Aesop's fables, with their all-too-human animal characters in allegorical situations, have been learned by most people in early childhood; whether at bedtime, in school or even in Bugs Bunny cartoons. Despite all their interpretations, the fables still retain their simple, humorous charm. The tales of others, like **Mother Goose,** the **Brothers Grimm** (see No. 20) and **Hans Christian Andersen**, have also had a lasting effect on children, but Aesop's fables were the first of their kind. Many of his stories are believed to have originated as far back as prehistoric times. Aesop would have recomposed them to represent his beliefs.

Like **Homer**'s epics (see No. 1), the stories are believed to have circulated orally, until they were recorded around 300 BC. In Hellenistic times, schoolboys studied his tales, while orators and philosophers used them to illustrate a point.

Aesop tells a fable.

Each fable contains a cautionary, ageless moral. "The Tortoise and the Hare" teaches that perseverance can be more valuable than skill, while "The Ant and the Grasshopper" illustrates that diligence has life-sustaining rewards.

The fables have also given us such popular expressions as the regretful "sour grapes" from "The Fox and the Grapes."

There is also the often-used phrase "a wolf in sheep's clothing," which comes from yet another fable in which Aesop tells of a wolf disguises himself as a sheep in order to get into a flock of sheep grazing in a meadow.

3. VIRGIL
70-19 BC

Known as **Virgil** (or Vergel), his full name was **Publius Vergilius Maro**. A Roman poet and author of the *Aeneid*, he was born in 70 BC at Andes, near Mantua, in Cisalpine Gaul. His education, begun in Cremona, continued in Mediolanum (now Milan), and was completed in Rome. He planned to practice law, but after one unimpressive appearance in court, the modest, timid young man returned to his farm and began to write, only to be evicted. In 41 BC, Antony's veterans, home from the Philippi campaign, were rewarded with the customary allotment of land.

In 19 BC he went to Athens with the idea of completing his final revision of the *Aeneid*. When Augustus appeared in the city and urged him to return to Rome, he gathered up his still unfinished manuscript and joined the imperial party. Before the ship reached Italy he fell ill and he died at Brundisium (modern Brindisi).

A furious argument has raged for many years over a group of poems collectively called *Appendix Vetgiliana* and ascribed to Virgil. It is highly probable that some of his early poetic efforts are to be found in this collection. However, he certainly did not write all of the pieces. In 37 BC he published his *Bucolics* or *Eclogues*. His model was Theocritus, whose *Idylls* were composed about 270 BC. The most interesting of the *Bucolics* is the fourth, which proclaims the coming of a golden age, to be heralded by the birth of a divine child. For many centuries Virgil was believed to have prophesied, in this lovely poem, the birth of Jesus.

During Virgil's stay in Naples, he wrote the *Georgics*, a work of surpassing beauty. Composed at the suggestion of Maecenas, its purpose was to aid and support Augustus in the promotion of a back-to-the-country movement. The four books deal respectively with agriculture, horticulture, the rearing of farm animals, and beekeeping. In the fourth book, the poet tells us that if "he were not near the end of his task and the furling of his sails, he would sing of gardens."

The last 11 years of Virgil's life were devoted to the *Aeneid*, an epic in 12 books illustrating the fall of Troy, the wanderings of Aeneas and ideals of classical beauty. In a Trojan settlement in Latium, Virgil casts himself in the role of imperial propagandist. Venus is the mother of Aeneas, and Idlus, his son, is the progenitor of the Julian line, which has now given to the world the great Augustus, its final and perfect flower. Meanwhile, Rome's divine mission as ruler of the races of men is proclaimed with evangelical fervor and passion.

Many readers consider Book VI the most beautiful and impressive of the 12. Here we read of the descent of the hero into Hades, where he finds the shade of his father Anchises in the Elysian Fields and receives encouragement and counsel for the tempestuous days that lie ahead.

Virgil.

4. LI PO
701-762

The great Chinese poet **Li Po** (or **Li Tai Po**) was born to a family of minor nobility in the province of Szechwan. He was attached for some time to the Imperial Court of the Tang Dynasty. Under Li Po's patron, Emperor Hsuan Tsung, China experienced a golden age in terms of art and literature.

Hsuan Tsung, who was known as Ming Huang, the "Brilliant Emperor," created an environment in which writers and authors could live and flourish, and Li Po was joined at the royal court by other poets, including the great **Tu Fu.**

By 750, however, Li Po tired of the bustled activity in the palace and decided to travel throughout China and experience life in rural ares and small towns. Most of his remaining life was spent wandering about with "the Eight Immortals of the Wine Cup," a roving band of drunken poets. It should be noted that the numeral "eight" is important in Chinese literature and art, appearing in "The Eight Basic Strokes," and "The Eight Trigrams."

According to legend, Li Po drowned during a drinking bout when he tried to embrace the reflection of the moon in the Yellow River.

Whatever can be said of his lifestyle and the embarrassing way he died, Li Po was a great poet, whose writing have been influential to Chinese literature. The purity, subtlety and conciseness of his intimate, hedonistic lyrics have rarely been equaled. He is commonly described as the greatest Chinese poet. There are English translations of the poems by **Shigeyoshi Obata** (*Works of Li Po*) and Florence Ayscough and Amy Lowell (*Fir-Flower Tablets*).

Li Po.

5. OMAR KHAYYAM
1048-1131

A Persian poet and astronomer, **Omar Khayyam** was born in Nishapur, Khorassan around 1048, and died in 1123 or 1131. When offered wealth by a lifelong friend, he is noted to have declined the gift, answering: "The greatest boon you can confer on me is to let me live in a corner under the shadow of your fortune, to spread wide the advantages of science, and pray for your long life and prosperity." So he lived "busied in winning knowledge of every kind."

His Takhallus, or poetical name (Khayyam), means "tentmaker," and he is noted at one time to have exercised that trade. As an astronomer he was responsible for a revision of the Persian calendar, and occupied a position of importance at the court of the Sultan Malik Shah at Merv. He wrote a number of works on mathematics, in which one on algebra, was translated by Woepeke (1851). It is, however, as the author of a collection of quatrains, called the *Rubaiyat*, that Omar Khayyam is more popularly known. These poems, isolated, impulsive, unrestrained, and characterized by rapid transitions from minstrelsy of love and grave argument to deadly fatalism and ribald tavern song, demonstrate an interesting development of Persian mysticism. As with the Song of Solomon, these poems are interpreted in literal context, as well as figuratively.

The *Rubaiyat* was practically unknown in the West until the publication of an English translation by **Edward FitzGerald** in 1859. Three subsequent editions were published during FitzGerald's life (1868, 1872, 1879), and a fifth edition was included in *The Letters and Literary Remains of Edward Fitzgerald,* edited by W. A. Wright (1889).

Numerous editions have appeared since. FitzGerald's work has been called a "poetic transfusion" rather than a translation. He rearranged the quatrains to produce a sequence of thought not evident in Khayyam's work, and there is even doubt as to Omar's authorship of some of the verses. Other translations into English have been made by E. H. Whinfield, who followed the original much more closely than FitzGerald; by Justin Huntley McCarthy, whose version, though in prose, has all the qualities that are generally termed poetic; by Edward Heron Allen, whose translation is also in prose, closely following the original; by John Leslie Garner; by John Payne; and by Jesse E. Cadell.

Omar Khayyam.

The Italian poet, **Dante Alighieri**, whose *Divine Comedy* ranks as one of the world's great literary works, was born in Florence in 1265. He has come to be known by his first name Dante, a shortened form of Duranto. He attended universities in Florence, Bologna, and Padua, where he eagerly studied drawing, as well as natural and moral philosophy. His writings indicate that he had read the *Summa Theologica* of St. Thomas Aquinas, and was an astute political thinker, participating actively in the public life of Florence. Around 1296 he married Gemma dei Donati, a relative of Corso Donati, a Black Guelf leader and Dante's political opponent.

In his writings, Dante was concerned with helping men to "attain that knowledge which shall lead them into the paths of righteousness."

Dante Alighieri.

The *Divine Comedy*, an allegory, has been hailed as the first Christian poem. In it, Dante is guided by the Roman poet Virgil through Hell (*Inferno*), Purgatory (*Purgatorio*), and ultimately Heaven (*Paradisio*), where he described having "observed" the punishments and rewards of earthly behavior and wrote about having seen many recently-deceased celebrities and Florentine notables.

In 1300, he was elected to the Florence city council, but in 1302 Dante, along with five other citizens, was condemned for crimes of barratry and offenses against the Guelf party. His real and only offense, however, had been opposition to the policies of Pope Boniface VIII. Dante believed that the papacy should be concerned only with spiritual matters. He was banished from Florence under penalty of being burned alive should he ever return.

Immediately after his banishment, Dante joined hundreds of other Florentine exiles at a castle near Arezzo. They allied themselves with Bianchi forces and tried several times, unsuccessfully, to force an entry into Florence. Dante's pleas for pardon were all refused. For the rest of his life, Dante roamed through Italy. In his wanderings, he described himself as "a bark without sail and without rudder, borne to diverse ports and bays and shores by that dry wind which grievous poverty breathes forth."

The Banquet, written sometime after his banishment, perhaps 1303, was intended as a handbook of universal knowledge; the *Vita Nuova*, a poem of his youth, is a lyric eulogy of Beatrice, a leading character in the *Comedy*, whose identity is still subject to controversy.

Dante's minor works include *De Monarchia, De Vulgari Eloquenta, Questis de Aqua et Terra,* and *Eclogues.* A few of his letters have also been preserved.

It is probable that he spent his last years at Ravenna, under the protection of Guido da Polenta, a philosopher-poet and lord of the city. He died there in July or September, 1321, not long after the completion of his immortal *Divine Comedy.*

7. GIOVANNI BOCCACCIO
1313-1375

Giovanni Boccaccio, the son of a French woman and a Florentine banker, was born in Paris. His youth was spent in Tuscany, but his earliest works were written in Naples, where he was a member of King Robert's literary circle.

A romance with **Maria d'Aquino**, the king's illegitimate daughter, inspired *Filocolo* (c. 1339), his first and longest novelette, and the *Teseide* (1340), the source of Geoffrey Chaucer's *Knight's Tale*.

The *Ameto, Amorosa Visione* and *Fiammetta*, written in Florence (1341-1344), were also connected with his Neapolitan mistress. The *Decamerone*, on which his fame rests, was completed between 1348 and 1353. It consists of 100 tales related in ten days by a party of seven women and three men who took refuge in a villa near Florence to escape the plague that was raging in that city.

After 1350, Boccaccio was closely associated with **Petrarch** in humanistic research. The fruits of Boccaccio's association with Petrarch are an assortment of works in Latin which reveal an almost religious devotion to humanistic ideals. Following his conversion to the classical tradition, he began an extensive program of reading. The results of his "sacred studies," essentially compilations of notes on his reading, are represented in such works as *De montibus, sylvis, fontibus, lacubus, fluminibus, stagnis et paludibus, et de nominibus maris*, a geographical compendium; *De genealogiis decorum gentilium* (1350-60), a summary of mythological lore; and two collections of moralistic biography; *De claris mulieribus* (1352-62) and *De casibus virorum et feminarum illustrium* (1363).

A more significant monument to his industrious humanism is Leon Pilatus' translation, through which the work was first restored to the canon of European culture. Giovanni Boccaccio's discerning patronage of the Byzantine scholar inspired the attention of Pilatus.

Petrarch had originally commissioned the translation, but his interest in Greek letters was as shallow as his knowledge of the language. After a brief fit of enthusiasm, he abandoned the project.

Boccaccio received the vagrant humanist into his own home, encouraged him to complete the work, and secured his appointment as professor of Greek language and literature at the University of Florence.

English versions of tales from the *Decameron* appeared in William Painter's *The Palace of Pleasure* (1566-1567), but the first complete translation was published in 1620.

Giovanni Boccaccio.

FRANCOIS RABELAIS
1494?-1553

Francois Rabelais was born in Chinon and studied at Fontenay-le-Comte, where Greek studies under Bude directed his interest toward humanism. His friends included were **Pierre Amy, Geoffroy d'Estissac,** and **Andre Tiraqueau**.

Having received his baccalaureate in medicine at Montpellier (1530), he lectured on the Aphorisms of Hippocrates and the *Ars Medico* of Galen. While serving as physician at the Pont du Rhone Hospital at Lyons, Rabelais wrote a remarkable letter to **Erasmus** (1532).

At Lyons, the avowed center of the French Renaissance, Rabelais began his great work which made him "the founder of modern French prose." The protagonists of the narrative, the giants Gargantua and Pantagruel, continue their adventures through five books: *Pantagruel* (1532), *Gargantua* (1535), the *Third Book* (1546), the *Fourth Book* (1552), and the *Fifth Book* (1562).

Pantagruel's eulogy of Debt, and Gargantua's letter to his son, sometimes called "the triumphal hymn of the Renaissance," voice the liberated intelligence of the age.

Rabelais was a skillful and successful physician. He edited Galen and Hippocrates. However, his dissection of a cadaver is more consistent with his empiricism and more significant to medical history.

He believed that life should be lived to the fullest, both on the physical and the intellectual planes. He felt that all that frustrates or mutilates nature is evil.

In his earlier work, Rabelais appears sympathetic to the religious reformers, yet in *Book III* he flays "the demoniac Calvinists." Rabelais' style, as buoyantly exuberant as life itself, "overflows his page."

Rabelais made at least three visits to Rome in the service of his patron the Cardinal Jean du Bellay (1534, 1535, 1549). During his final stay, he wrote *La Sciomachie*, a

Francois Rabelais.

series of letters describing his patron's celebration of the birth of the Duke of Orleans.

The hostility of the Sorbonne, roundly satirized in *Book I*, doubtless accounts for his prolonged absence from the Lyons hospital and his temporary replacement in 1535.

After Rabelais' appointment as curate of Meudon by du Bellay (1551), the publication of the *Fourth Book*, condemned by the Sorbonne and by Parliament, again placed him in jeopardy. He soon resigned his charge and there is no further account of his activities.

In Rabelais' opinion, life was the greatest teacher, experience the eternal solvent. Rabelaisian realism, wholesome and sane, inspired the common sense of Montaigne and Moliere.

Rabelais reasoned that in the pursuit of the aim there is no medievalism, no asceticism in the sublime freedom of the Abbey of Thelema: "Do as thou wilt."

The great Spanish novelist, poet, and dramatist, **Miguel de Cervantes** was born at Alcala de Henares. He was educated under the famous humanist Juan Lopez de Hoyos. On the arrival of Cardinal Giulio Acquaviva in Madrid (1568), Cervantes was appointed to an office in the Papal nuncio's household to console Philip II on the loss of his son Don Carlos. In this post, he accompanied his master to Rome.

Leaving this service in 1570, Cervantes spent the next five years as a soldier. In the naval Battle of Lepanto (1571), his left hand was permanently injured, earning him the nickname of *el manco de Lepanto*. He continued fighting against the Turks until 1575, when he sailed from Naples to Spain, but he was captured at sea by pirates. After his release in 1582, he returned to Madrid, where he settled down to a career of writing.

Cervantes' best-known poetical work is the *Galatea*, a pastoral narrative tale, first published in 1585. Although the prose of Cervantes has overshadowed his poetry, of which he was so proud, there are verses of great beauty in the *Galatea*, and in *El Viage al Parnaso*.

As a dramatist Cervantes worked hard, though unsuccessfully, and only he himself thought highly of his plays. In the *Adjunto al Parnaso* he enumerates those of his dramas which he considers the best among the number, *El Trato de Argel, La Numancia,* and *La Conjusa,* of which the last named is perhaps the best.

It is, however, as a novelist that Cervantes has become immortal. Successive writers have endeavored to discover in *Don Quixote* a great philosophical satire, but the truth of Cervantes' own assurance is now generally admitted. His sole desire was to write an amusing book to give the *coup de grace* to the absurd books of chivalry imitating Amadis that had done so much to

Miguel de Saavedra Cervantes.

give a bad name to Spanish literature. The book must have been started later than 1591, but the suggestion that he wrote it in a jail in Argamasilla de Alba rests on interpretation of a remark made by Cervantes in the prologue. In any case, it was famous in manuscript form for some time before a license was granted in 1604 to print the first part.

The book seems to have been first sold at the beginning of the year 1605. Lope de Vega wrote slightingly of it shortly before; but the public read it with avidity. Five (or six, if there really was a Barcelona edition of 1605) editions appeared before the end of 1605.

In 1613, Cervantes issued his twelve *Novelas Exemplares*, short stories written at considerable intervals. Abounding in wit and vivacity, rivaling even *Don Quixote* itself, they have maintained their popularity to the present day. Cervantes' last work was *Los Trabajos de Persilesy Sigismunda*, written in 1616, and dedicated to the Count de Lemos, was signed four days before the author's death.

An English dramatist, **Christopher Marlowe** was born in Canterbury, the son of a shoemaker. He graduated from Corpus Christi College, Cambridge in 1583, earning his master's degree in 1587. He went directly from the university to London to make his way in the theater. In any event, during the late 1580s and early 1590s, he was perhaps the most talented of the group of writers known as "The University Wits." Their work revolutionized Elizabethan drama during these years and paved the way for the great dramatists of the next two decades.

His work was the single greatest influence on **William Shakespeare** (see No. 11), who made one of his rare overt personal references to Marlowe.

The chronology of Marlowe's work has not been definitely established, but *Tamberlaine* (1587), probably comes first. Like all Marlowe's work, this play is concerned with what is perhaps the major conflict of the Renaissance mind; the clash between reason and faith.

Tamberlaine takes the side of reason, presenting with epic enthusiasm the rise from Scythian shepherd to "the sweet fruition of an earthly crown" of Tamberlaine. He achieved this distinction, not because he was born to it, nor because he was God's anointed, but because he used his great personal talents, with ruthless disregard for others.

Marlowe's second play, *The Tragical History of Doctor Faustus* (1588), was certainly the greatest tragedy before Shakespeare. It achieved this stature by balancing Marlowe's admiration for the man ambitious of power, knowledge, and beauty with the powerful conviction that a man who achieved these ends, not by God's gift, but by the unaided efforts of his intelligence and will, used damnable means. *Doctor Faustus* is an example of the Renaissance humanist. At the end of Marlowe's play he was damned.

Doctor Faustus was probably followed by *The Jew of Malta* (1589-90) and *Edward II* (1591), from which Shakespeare borrowed extensively for Richard II. Marlowe certainly had some part in several other plays, and, in addition, was a considerable lyric poet.

His most famous non-dramatic poem is the unfinished *Hero and Leander*. He died in a tavern brawl, perhaps deliberately murdered, at the age of 29.

Christopher Marlowe.

WILLIAM SHAKESPEARE
1564-1616

Revered for generations as possibly the greatest writer in the English language, **William Shakespeare** was a poet, playwright, and actor. He was born in Stratford-upon-Avon where he spent his childhood and youth. After he had become a successful dramatist and a wealthy businessman, he retired to it.

Soon after he left school, Shakespeare married **Anne Hathaway**, then he probably went to London to seek his fortune, where he managed to get a minor job in the theater and learned the art of acting. The company of players he joined is not known. He may have connected with more than one, but the most probable company was that which had as its patron the Earl of Pembroke.

Shakespeare became a competent actor. A contemporary witness told that he played the parts of kings. It is also felt by some scholars that he reserved for himself such roles as Adam in *As You like It* and as the ghost in *Hamlet*.

Shakespeare also learned to write plays. By 1592, he was quite successful. Those of his early period include *The Comedy of Errors, Titus Andronicus,* and *Henry VI*, Parts 1, 2, and 3. Similar themes followed in *Richard III* and *Henry VII*. From 1592, the theaters were closed almost continuously for two years because of the bubonic plague.

Shakespeare turned his attention to narrative poetry, which was considered by his fellow Elizabethans as serious literature, to contrast with the drama. His *Venus and Adonis* met with an immediate success, so great indeed that Shakespeare followed it with another long poem, *The Rape of Lucrece*.

About this time, Shakespeare also began writing a series of 154 poems, all but three of them 14-line sonnets. The composition of these sonnets was spread over a number of years.

In 1594, he returned to drama with a series of comedies, including *The Taming of the Shrew*, a rollicking story of how a young husband changed his nagging, domineering bride into a sweet-tempered and dutiful wife.

Others included *Two Gentlemen of Verona, Love's Labour's Lost* and *A Midsummer Night's Dream*, in which he first made use of the supernatural, which he later employed so successfully in *Macbeth, Hamlet, The Tempest,* and *The Merchant of Venice*. Around 1600 Shakespeare wrote the comedies *Much Ado About Nothing, As You Like It* and *Twelfth Night*.

Shakespeare did not restrict himself during this period entirely to comedies. Indeed, Shakespeare's comic art probably reached its greatest height in two of the histories, *Henry IV*, Part 2 and the character, Sir John Falstaff, is one of his greatest.

He described the death of the intriguing old rascal in *Henry V*, perhaps the greatest of his historical plays. This story of the conquest of France by England's hero-king appealed to the patriotic feelings of his audience, with scenes of the battle of Agincourt. Shakespeare brought Falstaff back to life to become the hero of *The Merry Wives of Windsor*, Shakespeare's only picture of contemporary English middle-class life. In this comedy, Falstaff assails the virtue of two middle-aged small-town women with disastrous consequence to himself.

During this period, Shakespeare also wrote *Richard II*, the story of a weakling who lost his throne. *King John* was a less successful play. King John, who had been forced to grant the Magna Carta did not appeal to a dramatist who admired the semi-absolutism of Elizabeth.

Shakespeare also wrote two tragedies during this period: one at the beginning of it, the other at its end. *Romeo and Juliet*, written around 1594, is the story of two

"star-crossed lovers" the son and daughter of two quarreling families whose enmity brings death to their young children. *Julius Caesar*, written around 1599, is the story of a political assassination and the national disaster of civil war which followed it.

While he was writing these comedies, histories, and tragedies, Shakespeare was achieving success as an actor and was growing in wealth. He desired, like many other middle-class men of his time, to be granted a coat of arms. This would entitle him to be styled "gentleman" and to occupy the rank in society next below a knight. On October 20, 1596, heralds granted John Shakespeare and his children a coat of arms, the chief element of which is a falcon shaking a spear. The next year, 1597, Shakespeare purchased New Place, one of the largest houses in Stratford.

William Shakespeare.

In 1599 he joined with a group that included four of his fellow actors to build a theater in Southwark, on the bank of the Thames. With a capacity of about 1,500 people, it was the largest theater in England. It was named "**The Globe**" from the sign painted above its door; a picture of Atlas holding the world on his shoulders. Shakespeare now was part owner of a theater in which he acted, and he sometimes appeared there in plays which he himself had written. This combination was quite profitable for the owner, actor, and playwright.

It is strange to find Shakespeare, at the height of his success, changing from the comedies which he had been writing for about seven years to tragedies and to darkly serious comedies.

Around 1599, Shakespeare wrote his greatest drama, probably the greatest tragedy ever written, *Hamlet, Prince of Denmark*. In this play, the ghost of Hamlet's father reveals to Hamlet that it is his duty to avenge his murder; that he had been poisoned by his brother, who desired his throne and his queen. Hamlet hesitates to kill his own uncle, and by delaying brings death on his beloved Ophelia, her family, his mother, and himself.

His last great tragedies included *Othello, the Moor of Venice*, *Macbeth*, and *Antony and Cleopatra*. All of them rank among his greatest works. His other plays were *Coriolanus* and *Timon of Athens*.

William Shakespeare died at New Place, Stratford, on April 23, 1616, and was buried in a place of honor by the high altar in the Stratford church. An expensive monument bearing his bust was placed above his grave. Shakespeare wrote 39 plays, including those in which he collaborated.

12. JOHN BUNYAN
1628-1688

Labeled for many years as a "nonconformist," **John Bunyan** was born the son of a tinker in Elitow in Bedfordshire, England. In 1644, he enlisted in the Parliamentary army, serving a year in England and perhaps another year in Ireland. As a result, military language is present throughout his writings.

In 1646, he married a very religious woman and abandoned his "sins" of blasphemy, dancing on the green, and ringing the church bells. The outward reformation was followed by a long and difficult struggle against the sense of "sin," aggravated by despondency and melancholia.

Finally winning the struggle, Bunyan, like his father, a tinker by trade, began a career as a religious writer. In 1660 he became a dissenting preacher and was imprisoned for 12 years. He refused to free himself by choosing to remain in the ministry.

As a preacher, Bunyan was indefatigable and immensely popular; never failing to draw a huge crowd of listeners.

His literary career, which had begun in 1656 with *Some Gospel Truths Opened*, continued until his death. In all, close to 60 of his works in prose and meter have been published.

His chief fame rests on *Pilgrim's Progress* (1678), which was largely added to in the second and third editions. This allegory of an ordinary man making his way to heaven is one of the most influential books in Western civilization.

The second part (1684) is noted to be considerably weaker and and lacking the innovation of the first part. *The Life and Death of Mr. Badman* (1680) is intended to be a contrast to *Pilgrim's Progress. Grace Abounding to the Chief of Sinners* (1666), is autobiographical, but overstates the wickedness of the author. *The Holy War* (1682), a powerful work, has been overshadowed by *Pilgrim's Progress.*

John Bunyan.

13. DANIEL DEFOE
1660-1731

The most important pioneer in the development of the English novel, **Daniel Defoe,** was born in London in 1660. The son of Presbyterian parents, he attended the Dissenting School in Newington Green. After a short career in business, he turned to journalism, and from 1697 to 1719 established himself as one of England's foremost journalists. During these years he wrote *An Essay upon Projects* (1697), notable for its advanced views on education, insurance, and the treatment of seamen.

The True-Born Englishman (1701), was a satire in verse, in which he ridiculed the Englishman's contemptuous attitude toward the Dutch. *The Shortest Way with the Dissenters* (1702), was a bantering satire on the plans of the extreme High Church to persecute the Dissenters. For writing this, he was imprisoned, but later released.

From 1706 to 1710, Defoe, on orders from the London Ministry, spent most of his time in Scotland. Through his pamphlets and lobbying, he played an important part in the establishment of the Union. On his return to England, he was vigorously attacked by Whigs and Tories alike, for what appeared to them his rank treachery to both parties. Apparently undisturbed by these slurs on his political conduct, Defoe continued to keep the press busy with pamphlets.

From 1719 to 1728 Defoe devoted much of his time to the production of books; the best known of which may perhaps be described as realistic fiction. For this work he drew heavily on his experiences as a tradesman, journalist, inmate of Newgate, and traveler; and also on his wide knowledge of geography, recent history, and travel literature.

The outstanding work of this period is, of course, his masterpiece about survival and self-discovery on a deserted island. *Robinson Crusoe* (1719), still remains a favorite English classic of readers worldwide. His works include *Memoirs of a Cavalier* (1720), a pioneer work in historical fiction; *Moll Flanders* (1720) and *Colonel Jack* (1720) are realistic novels of low life; and *Journal of the Plague Year* (1722) is a masterly piece of historical imaginative writing. *A Tour Through the Whole Island of Great Britain* (1723-1725) is one of the most readable and informative of British guidebooks and *Roxana* (1724) is the story of a soulless wanton. The curious *Political History of the Devil* (1726) was clearly ahead of its time. *The Complete English Tradesman* (1727) is a classic example of Defoe's ability to make the subject of trade pleasant, as well as profitable reading. *Robert Drury's Journal* (1729), is in some respects, as entertaining as *Robinson Crusoe*. Alexander Pope once remarked: "Defoe wrote a vast many things; and none bad, though none excellent but this [*Robinson Crusoe*]. There is something good in all that he has written."

Daniel Defoe.

A satirist, as well as a churchman, **Jonathan Swift** was born of English parents in Dublin, Ireland. He was personally ambitious, but because of a combination of circumstances and animosities, the highest position he received was the deanship of St. Patrick's University in Dublin (1713). He held the post and administered with constancy and effectiveness for 22 years.

All of Swift's literary works appeared anonymously. His first masterpiece, *A Tale of a Tub* (written in 1697, published in 1704), was an excruciatingly amusing satirical fable of the abuses of religion, interspersed episodically, and framed with ironical critiques and parodies of the absurdities of literature. He developed this theme further in his mock-epic *Battle of the Books*, which can be seen as Swift's contribution to the critical *War of the Ancients and the Moderns*, in which he sides with the former.

Jonathan Swift.

Swift's most popular work will always remain *Gulliver's Travels* (composed in 1721-1725, published in 1726). It is the amazing tale of the voyages to Lilliput and Brobdingnag, the lands of pygmies and giants, that is a perennial favorite with children, and an incomparable adventure story. The four voyages together comprise the most devastating satire of human nature ever written, but contain antidotes which prove Swift far from the misanthrope, pessimist, and cynic he is commonly labeled to be by superficial readers. All four contain Utopian elements, culled from experience or inferred from the application of reason to human problems. The third voyage is ordinarily misinterpreted as ridicule of legitimate science. It is merely an exposure of pseudoscientific folly, the harebrained "projects" of dodderers, and the amateurish dabbling of scientists in governmental activities for which they are not qualified. The loathsome Yahoos of the fourth voyage can only be correctly understood, not as men, but as allegorical embodiments of degenerate depravity unredeemed by reason. The Houyhnhnms are not really horses, but "the perfection of nature," i.e., human nature when controlled by reason. Actual men, as Gulliver describes their doings, sink lower than Yahoos when they use reason for irrational ends, as in war. Into all four voyages, especially the first and third, Swift introduced fascinating materials of satiric political allegory.

The special qualities of his work are coming to be justly prized by readers not rigidly bound by Romantic and Victorian definitions and standards of poetry. He was a man of strange paradoxes, but to children, as to adults who fully understand his work, he was a lovable man, and irresistibly cynical in his sense of irony.

Born **Francois Marie Arouet** in 1694, **Voltaire** was the son of a well educated Parisian notary, and in turn descended from "respectable" bourgeois people. Voltaire competed for poetry prizes, satirized the Academy, and won approval of the liberal element. Early satirical writings finally earned him 11 months imprisonment in the Bastille in 1717. Released by the regent, he experienced his first dramatic success in the tragedy *Oedipe*.

Voltaire spent more time in jail as a result of his challenge to the Chevalier de Rohan-Chabot, who incited his thugs to assault the young poet in the street in 1725. This was followed by more than two years voluntary exile in England (1726-1729), where he visited **Alexander Pope, Jonathan Swift** (see No.14), **John Locke** and **Sir Isaac Newton**. After his time spent in England, Voltaire's skepticism, cosmopolitanism, and dramatic technique were revitalized. In the meantime, his popular epic *La Henriade* (1728-1730), began to appear. The semi-Shakespearian *Zaire* (1732), brought its author much glory.

Also written in this period were the *Histoire de Charles XII* (1731), and the *Temple du Gout*, a satire after the manner of Pope. The *Lettres Philosophiques* (1734), which attacked stupid despotism by praising English tolerance, cost Voltaire another exile. He fled to Cirey on the Lorraine border, where for 14 years he was to live as the guest of Madame du Chatelet.

Zaire and *Mirope* which are probably his best tragedies, were followed by his *Dictionnaire Philosophique* (1764) which was an intellectual battery aimed at contemporary religion. Voltaire, like Descartes, based God in part on the necessity for rationalizing conscious existence.

He saw too clearly the role of chance in human affairs to believe in the conventional Providence. His philosophical fiction is well represented by *Candide* (1759).

The death of Madame du Chatelet in 1749, was the greatest sorrow of his life. He dedicated his remaining years to the battle against political oppression, superstition, and religious intolerance. After a long absence his return to Paris in 1778 was the occasion of endless rejoicing and celebration. Enfeebled in health, Voltaire died a literal victim of his own renown. His tireless energy was wrested from a lifetime of ill health. In 1791 the Revolutionists deposited his body in the Pantheon.

Voltaire (Francois Marie Arouet).

16. WILLIAM BLAKE
1757-1827

Born in London, **William Blake** was the son of an Irishman. Early in life he was apprenticed to an engraver, studied at the Royal Academy, and made his living by engraving illustrations for London publishers. Often he was poor, and almost never was he fully appreciated by the other writers of his time. Blake is now regarded as one of the most sophisticated figures in the history of both poetry and art.

Like the other Romantic era poets, Blake looked at nature with fresh, inquiring eyes. He found mystery and beauty in life itself. His writings and his art alike remained extremely individual, even among the individualistic Romantic poets. One important characteristic of his writing is his dependence on symbols so complicated that they have been clearly and entirely understood by few of his readers.

Blake's early poems are remarkably childlike and simple. The best known of his poems are found in *Songs of Innocence*, published in 1789, and in *Songs of Experience*, published five years later. Every schoolchild has been taught *The Tyger* which begins "Tyger! Tyger! burning bright, in the forests of the night."

In his "Introduction" to the *Songs of Innocence*, he writes:

"Piping down the valleys wild, Piping songs of pleasant glee, On a cloud I saw a child, And he laughing said to Me."

Blake's fierce love of animals, as well as children, is shown in his poem, "Auguries of Innocence," which contains the lines, "A Robin Red Breast in a Cage, Puts all Heaven in a Rage."

This feeling for children and animals sprang from his violent love of liberty; a love that tended toward anarchism. He welcomed the French Revolution and accepted its political ideals.

Blake's first book of poems was printed in 1783, and included poems written when he was a teenager. Later books, such as *Milton* and *Jerusalem* were published with engravings, some of them hand colored, from Blake's own designs. In these, the text and the engravings were intended to be a unified whole, to be read and interpreted together. In 1790, Blake's principal work in prose and pictures, *The Marriage of Heaven and Hell,* attacked the reality of matter and denied the rights of authority. Other of Blake's work, such as *Vala* and *The Four Zoas,* are filled with complex characters and mystical ideas.

Blake also illustrated the major writings of other authors. His illustrations for the *Book of Job* from the Old Testament and for **Dante**'s *Divine Comedy* (see No. 6) are considered to be masterpieces.

William Blake.

ROBERT BURNS
1759-1796

Scotland's most popular poet, **Robert "Robbie" Burns**, grew up near Mauchline, where he encountered the *Poems of Robert Fergusson.* Through Fergusson's work, Burns first realized the literary possibilities of the Scots vernacular. His first such essay was "The Two Herds," a satire on a dispute then raging between two "Auld Licht" (conservative) ministers.

In 1786, Burns published his *Poems, Chiefly in the Scottish Dialect*, which had immediate success. When copies reached **Dugald Stewart, James, Earl of Glencairn**, and other men of influence, they arranged for a second printing in Edinburgh.

Burns was patronized by the gentry, who, unaware of the real extent of his reading and study, hailed him as a "Bard of Nature." Some of these people, however, were offended by the poet's occasionally blunt speech and by his ignorance of the finer points of etiquette.

Burns had hoped for an appointment in the tax service and returned to farming almost in desperation after his patrons had failed to help him. At the last moment, though, he obtained authorization to receive Excise Instructions. With his commission in his pocket, he began work at Ellisland and acknowledged Jean Armour as his wife, after she had already borne him two sets of twins.

The farm went badly. Burns soon turned to the Excise to supplement his income, and in November 1791, surrendered his lease and moved into Dumfries. For the remaining five years of his life he was wholly dependent on his salary. The third edition of his *Poems* (1793), brought him no profits, since he had been so ill-advised as to sell his copyright in 1787.

Burns' later poetry was produced in the intervals of farm and tax work. He wrote few additional satires, epistles, and dramatic monologues, as the famed Kilmarnock

Robert Burns.

volume. His one important long poem after the Edinburgh period was *Tam O'Shanter*, but it was his greatest. It was written at the urging of Captain Francis Grose (1731-1791), who wanted a witch story to accompany his engraving of Alloway Kirk in his *Antiquities of Scotland (1791).*

To such collections as James Johnson's *Museum*, George Thonsson's *Select Collection of Original Scottish Airs* (1793), and Peter Urbani's *Selection of Scots Songs* Burns contributed more than 300 songs, including some of the finest lyrics in the language. In these lyrics, **W.E. Henley** writes, Burns "passed the folk-song of his nation through the mint of his mind, and he reproduced it stamped with his image and lettered with his superscription; so that for the world at large it exists, and will go on existing, not as he found it but as he left it."

The great English poet **William Wordsworth** was born in the little town of Cockermouth in Cumberland, in northwest England. His father was an attorney, and his mother, Anne Cookson, was the daughter of a merchant. Both parents died before Wordsworth was 17, but they left an involved estate and the orphaned family was largely dependent on unsympathetic relatives. Wordsworth attended St. John's College, Cambridge, and later went on a walking tour of France, where the French Revolution excited his political passions. In 1792, Wordsworth fell in love with Annette Vallon, but he left France and didn't see his daughter Caroline until she was ten.

In 1793, Wordsworth published *An Evening Walk* and *Descriptive Sketches*, poems about nature. He responded to the political and ethical ideas of William Godwin, and under their influence wrote *Guilt and Sorrow,* and a grim poetic drama, *The Borderers.*

Living with his sister in a cottage in Dorsetshire until 1797, he formed a friendship with **Samuel Taylor Coleridge**. Wordsworth even wrote a few lines which remain in the text of *The Rime of the Ancient Mariner*, but Coleridge's more theoretic mind had a much more effective impact on Wordsworth's. In 1798, in the *Lyrical Ballads, Ancient Mariner* appeared between the same covers with Wordsworth's *Tintern Abbey.*

The unconventional simplicity of the language and the choice of realistic situations from common rural life, the collection challenged established standards of poetry. For a long time Wordsworth and Coleridge were to be pursued by an enthusiasm which began over *Lyrical Ballads.* It was to explain and justify his unconventionality that Wordsworth wrote his most famous prose composition, the *Preface* to the second edition of the *Ballads* (1800).

By 1798, Wordsworth's enthusiasm for the revolutionary cause had waned. There were many reasons for his shift, but the decisive factor appeared to have been the aggressive foreign policy of France in the invasion of Switzerland. Wordsworth has surveyed the development of his character and opinions in *The Prelude*, a very long, autobiographical poem in blank verse, extending through 14 books. This poem contains many of the finest passages of his works. It was begun before 1800, and he had a complete draft by 1805. The rest of his life he often took it up, rewrote it at least four times, and was constantly revising the successive drafts. The final draft, set down in 1839, was published in 1850, immediately after his death.

As a poetic work the final draft is perhaps superior to the draft of 1805, but the earliest draft is more precious as a revelation of the poet's mind and inner being; more dependable, and above all more forthright and candid.

William Wordsworth.

19. SIR WALTER SCOTT
1771-1832

Considered to be one of the greatest of the British Romantic era novelists, **Walter Scott** was born in Edinburgh, the son of Walter Scott the lawyer, and Anne Rutherford. Scott's literary interests began at an early age and ranged from Scottish history and folk ballads to the fashionable romanticism of Germany.

In 1805, Scott produced the immensely popular *Lay of the Last Minstrel*. It was, said critic **George Saintsbury**, with the exception of the Wordsworth and Coleridge lyrical ballads, "the first book published which was distinctly and originally characteristic of the new poetry of the nineteenth century." He followed the *Minstrel* with *Marmion* (1808), *The Lady of the Lake* (1810), *Rokeby* (1813), and *The Bridal of Triermain* (1813).

In 1813, he was offered the laureateship, but declined in favor of **Robert Southey**. During these same years, he edited the works of **John Dryden** (1808), and was active in the founding of the *Tory Quarterly Review* (1808-1809).

In 1814, Scott took up and completed a prose romance he had laid aside ten years prior. Published anonymously, as *Waverley*, the book achieved a popular success, surpassing even the narrative poems. After this work, he realized that he had almost exhausted his material, and that he could not compete with the more exotic verse of Byron. Among his great novels are *Guy Mannering* (1815), *The Antiquary* (1815), *The Black Dwarf* and *Old Mortality* (1816), *Rob Roy* (1817), *Heart of Midlothian* (1818), *The Bride of Lammermoor* and *Legend of Montrose* (1819), *Ivanhoe* (1820), *The Monastery* (1820), *The Abbott* (1820), *Kenilworth* (1821), *The Pirate* (1822), *The Fortunes of Nigel* (1822), *Peveril of the Peak* (1823), *Quentin Durward* (1823), *St. Ronan's Well* (1823), *Red Gauntlet* (1824), *Tales of the Crusaders: The Betrothed* and

Sir Walter Scott.

The Talisman (1825), and *Woodstock* (1826).

All were published anonymously. Scott denied authorship, though the matter was an open secret among his intimates, and was probably known to persons in authority when he was made a baronet in 1820. In 1820, also, he became president of the Royal Society of Scotland. In 1823 he became a member of the Roxburghe Club and founded the Bannatyne Club.

In 1826 Scott went bankrupt when a publishing venture in which he was involved failed. He promised to pay the debt from future book sales and was allowed to keep his home.

Scott composed a *Life of Napoleon* (1827), and novels and tales such as *Chronicles of the Canongate: The Two Drovers, The Highland Widow, The Surgeon's Daughter* (all, 1827), three series of *Tales of a Grandfather* (1828, 1829, 1830), *The Fair Maid of Perth* (1828), *Anne of Ceierstein* (1829), and *Count Robert of Paris* (1832). Scott's health broke under the strain. He suffered a paralytic stroke in 1830, and died two years later.

20. JACOB and WILHELM GRIMM
1785-1863, 1786-1859

The German philologists and folklorists **Jacob Ludwig Karl Grimm** and **Wilhelm Karl Grimm** were born in Hanau, the sons of a lawyer. They were educated at Marburg, where they studied law and acquired the antiquarian interests which were to motivate much of their work. In 1808, Jacob was appointed librarian to **Jerome Bonaparte**, king of Westphalia. In 1813, he became legation secretary and then Hessian ambassador at Paris. In 1816, he became librarian at the Kassel Library, where Wilhelm was already employed as secretary

During the rest of their lives, the brothers were closely associated, holding their property in common and collaborating intimately on such projects as the monumental *Deutsches Worterbuch* and the *Kinder und Hausmarchen* (1812, 1815), a collection of old German folk tales known to children the world over as *Grimm's Fairy Tales*.

Jacob published *Deutsche Grammatik* (1819), the second edition of which (1822) contains his formulation of the basic sound changes in Indo-European languages; *Deutsche Rechtsaltertumer* (1828), a survey of ancient Teutonic laws; *Deutsche Mythologie* (1835), in which he sought to relate the essential spirit of the German people to their primitive myths and customs. His vast *Geschichte der Deutschen Sprache* (1848), including not only a comprehensive study of the German language, but valuable observations on the general patterns of language evolution.

The Grimms held professorships at Gottingen for many years, but in 1837, Jacob joined in a plea to retain the Hanover constitution and was banished from the kingdom. They returned to Kassel for a few years, and in 1841, at the invitation of Friedrich Wilhelm IV, settled in Berlin as professors at the Royal University.

The importance of the Grimm brothers was the study of comparative linguistics, but most important was their landmark efforts in the successful preservation of central European folk legend.

Jacob Grimm and Wilhelm Grimm.

James Fenimore Cooper grew up in Lake Otsego, New York, where his father, Judge William Cooper, author of *A Guide in the Wilderness* (1810), had founded the frontier village of Cooperstown. Cooper describes his boyhood home, a bit of aristocracy on the fringe of the backwoods, in the first of his "Leather-Stocking Tales," *The Pioneers* (1823), and with less sympathy, in *Home as Found* (1838). He left college without graduating and spent several years aboard merchant ships and with the US Navy. From this came the books *The Pilot* (1823), and his scholarly and pioneering *History of the Navy of the United States of America* (1839). The *History* provoked bitter controversy over its treatment of the Battle of Lake Erie. After the failure of his first novel, *Precaution* (1820), he turned out five romances on American themes, starting with *The Spy* (1821), to prove that America could write as well as read literature.

James Fenimore Cooper.

His best work relies on his knowledge of the terrain of upstate New York and accounts of Native Americans. In his early novels, Cooper reveals an enthusiasm for the outdoors, dangerous action, and a consuming zeal for what he termed "American ideas." With the even greater success of *The Last of the Mohicans* (1826), perhaps the best and certainly the most widely popular of his Native American tales, his avocation as a novelist became his profession. He was the second American to make a success of a writing career. He followed Washington Irving to Europe in order to establish the English and Continental rights to his novels and to give his daughters the advantages of European schooling. While abroad, he wrote *Notions of the Americans* (1828), historical novels on European themes like *The Bravo* (1831), and further tales of Native Americans and the sea. By this time he had an international reputation, but disillusionment at the reception of his ideas at home produced a petulant tract, *A Letter to His Countrymen* (1834), in which he renounced the writing of fiction. These were followed with a political allegory, *The Monikins* (1835), his five volumes of travels (1836-1838), and a primer of his views, *The American Democrat* (1838). By 1841, he was to work on familiar themes with *The Pathfinder* and *The Deerslayer,* which with *The Prairie* (1827), completed the life story of his wilderness-hunter Natty Bumppo, or Leather-Stocking.

The best work of his mature years is a romantic trilogy, *Satanstoe* (1845), *The Chainbearer* (1845), and *The Redskins* (1846), in which he traces and defends the evolution of an American landed aristocracy through four generations. Among the sea novels of these years are *The Two Admirals* (1842), *Afloat and Ashore* (1844), and *The Sea Lions* (1849). *Wyandotte* (1843) and *The Oak Openings* (1848) were attempts to use the American backwoods in stories outside the frame of "The Leather-Stocking Tales." *The Crater* (1847) is his most thoughtful allegory of social and political criticism.

Born in Besancon, France, **Victor Hugo** was almost an infant prodigy, and at 23, he was one of the official poets of the French monarchy. The period from 1827 to 1842 was one of incredible activity and triumphs in every field for him. In poetry, he published *Odes and Ballads* (1822-26), *The Orientals* (1829), *Autumn Leaves* (1831), *Songs of Twilight* (1835), *Voices of the Innermost* (1837) and *Rays and Shadows* (1840). In the drama *Cromwell* he composed a masterly doctrinal preface (1827).

Other plays included *Hernani* (1830), the first performance of which was a big success for Hugo, *Marion Delorme* (1829-1831), *The King's Pleasure* (1832), and *Ruy Blas* (1838). In romance, *Notre-Dame de Paris* (1830) was an evocation of the medieval city and a defense of Gothic art.

Saddened by the tragic death of his favorite daughter and discouraged by the failure of his epic drama *Burgraves* (1843), Hugo abandoned literature for politics. Hugo, whose evolution was steadily toward the left, became a leader of the Radical Opposition, which led to his exile.

This exile opened for Victor Hugo a second career as a poet. He wrote *Chastisements* (1852), a political satire; *Contemplations* (1856); the mighty *Legend of the Centuries* (1859-1883); a vast collection of epic myths and episodes, with its weird and powerful prelude; *The End of Satan* (1886) and its philosophical conclusion *God* (1891). *God*'s range, power, and beauty, are unequaled in modern literature, and it is in sharp contrast to Hugo's airy *Songs of Streets and Woods* (1865). In the novel *Les Miserables* (1862) Hugo painted a great historical fresco and a powerful sermon, in the framework of a popular romance. *Toilers of the Sea* (1866), with fine descriptions and a symbol of evil (the octopus), is like **Herman Melville**'s *Moby Dick* (see No. 37). *The Man Who Laughs*, in which his riotous fantasy reached the limits of the baroque and even of the grotesque, is also notable.

Returning to France in 1871, he wrote *Ninety Three* (1873), a romance of the Revolution, and *The Four Winds of the Spirit* (1881), poems in lyrical, epic, satirical and dramatic form; being the best fruit of that almost juvenile productivity. A lover of children, he was revered as "the universal grandfather," publishing *The Art of Being a Grandfather* in 1877.

His funeral was an impressive ceremony. He lay in state under the Arch of Triumph, and the Pantheon was reopened to receive his remains. By the time of his centennial (1902), he was regarded as one of the major figures in world literature.

Baudelaire acknowledged his supremacy, **Alfred Tennyson** (see No. 28) called him "weird Titan, cloud-weaver of phantasmal hopes and fears," and **Andre Gide**, the very antithesis of Hugo, had to confess: "Our greatest poet, alas!" and in later years, withdrew the "alas!"

Victor Hugo.

A novelist and politician, **Edward George Earle Lytton Bulwer Lytton** (later First Baron Lytton) was born in London and educated at Cambridge, where he won the Chancellor's Medal for Poetry. The first work that brought him into prominence was his novel *Pelham*, published anonymously in 1828. His subsequent successes, such as *Eugene Aram* (1832), *The Last Days of Pompeii* (1834), *Rieni* (1835), and *Ernest Maltravers* (1837), brought him success and renown under his own name. *The Last Days of Pompeii* and *Rienzi* revealed Lytton's knack of holding the reader's interest in archeological and historical novels. Under Macready's management, and to some extent under his guidance, Lytton brought out at Drury Lane his own poetical play, *The Duchess of La Vallaire* (1836), with but small success. This was followed by the romantic comedy *The Lady of Lyons* (1838),

Edward Bulwer-Lytton.

which had a continued success on the stage; *Richelieu* (1839), a very popular historical-poetic drama, and *Money* (1840), which proved to be a highly remunerative comedy. Meanwhile, Lytton was achieving a reputation in the House of Commons, where he served as a Liberal member for St. Ives from 1831 to 1832, and for Lincoln from 1832 to 1841. He eventually returned to Parliament in 1852 as a Conservative, representing Hertfordshire until 1866, when he became a Lord.

Lytton continued to write fiction, the most popular examples being *Zanoni* (1842), *The Last of the Barons* (1843), *Lucretia* (1847), *Harold* (1848), *The Caxtons* (1849), *My Novel* (1853), *A Strange Story* (1862), *The Coming Race* (1871), *The Parissans* (1873), and *Kenelm Chillingly* (1873). He published several volumes of verse, notably the satiric *New Timon* (1846)

and *St. Stephen's* (1860), a romantic epic called *King Arthur* (1848-1849), and *The Lost Tales of Miletus* (1866).

Edward's son, **Edward Robert Bulwer**, First Earl of Lytton (1831-1891), was also an author and politician. Born in London and educated at Harrow, he wrote poetry under the name **Owen Meredith**, and earned a considerable literary reputation. Before succeeding to his father's title in 1873, he had widespread diplomatic experience at Washington and throughout Europe. In 1876 he became viceroy of India, where his administration was notable for his diplomatic services in connection with the Afghan War and for his energetic campaign against famine. He became Earl of Lytton in 1880, and was appointed ambassador at Paris in 1887, where he died suddenly. His best-known book was *Lucile* (1860), a long verse-narrative.

Descended from an old New England family which had been in Massachusetts since 1630, **Nathaniel Hawthorne** was born in Salem, Massachusetts. His first book, *Fanshawe* (1828), was a romantic fictional treatment based on his years at Bowdoin College. His short stories were collected and published in *Twice-Told Tales* (1837), only after Horatio Bridge had guaranteed that the publisher would not lose money by issuing the volume. They won little attention.

The year 1852 saw the publication of a collection of tales, *The Snow Image*, and a book-length narrative, *The Blithedale Romance*; the latter of which dealt in fictional form. Hawthorne's memories and impressions of Brook Farm. The same year, he wrote a campaign biography of his former college mate, **Franklin Pierce**. When Pierce was elected to the presidency, he appointed Hawthorne as consul to Liverpool (1853-1857). Between 1857 and 1860, the author and his family traveled in Italy and resided in England. His Italian travels furnished details utilized in *The Marble Faun* (1860). The year this novel appeared, he and his family returned to "The Wayside" in Concord. Hawthorne died at Plymouth, New Hampshire, while on a trip with ex-President Pierce.

Noteworthy in Hawthorne's tales and novels are certain themes and techniques. One theme frequently stressed is the undesirability of the isolation of the individual from his fellows. This theme, like others, is based on beliefs derived from Hawthorne's own experiences. Another interest of Hawthorne's which is important in his fiction was in the nature of sin and atonement.

During a period when many intellectuals in New England were **Unitarians** or **Transcendentalists**, Hawthorne tended to find validity in beliefs which many of his contemporaries had rejected; the beliefs of his Puritan ancestors. Although not a formal convert to Calvinism, this author, as Prof. Herbert W. Schneider remarked in The Puritan Mind, "saw the empirical truth behind the Calvinist symbols. He recovered what Puritans professed but seldom practiced, the spirit of piety, humility, and tragedy in the face of the inscrutable ways of God." Hence in "The Minister's Black Veil," "Young Goodman Brown" and other stories, Hawthorne told of the universal sinfulness of mankind. In *The Scarlet Letter*, of the need by the sinner for both penance and penitence; in *The Marble Faun*, of the genesis of sin; and in other narratives, of other aspects of sin and its expiation.

To develop his themes, Hawthorne cultivated a unique technique. As a boy, he had become acquainted with the writings of some of the great allegorists. Basing his method on suggestions derived from his reading of these authors, he located his stories, as he said, "in a neutral territory, somewhere between the real world and fairy land, where the Actual and the Imaginary may meet, and each imbue itself with the other."

Nathaniel Hawthorne.

Aurore Dupin was born in Paris in 1804, and spent her childhood at Nohant, in Berry. She studied for three years at the Convent des Anglaises in Paris, where she became involved in mysticism.

Returning to Nohant, she read Rousseau, Bernardin de Saint-Pierre, Chateaubriand, and other then-popular philosophers. When her marriage to Baron Dudevant ended in 1822, she returned to Paris to earn her living as a writer. She took the name **George Sand** as a *nom de plume*, because of her perception that women authors were not as marketable as men. Her novel *Indiana* (1832) first made famous the pseudonym she would use during 40 years of literary activity.

Her association with Alfred de Musset in an effort to "realize the ideal of Romantic love" inspired despairing notes in the poet's verse. In the novels *Valentine* (1832), *Lelia* (1833), *Jacques* (1834), and *Mauprat* (1837), the human heart is frequently at grips with the conventions of society.

Aurore Dupin wrote under the name George Sand.

Love is glorified as the eternal and exclusive passion, always hindered and handicapped by false social standards.

The mild and sentimental socialism of the decade 1840-1850 inspired *Consuelo* (1842-1843), *Le meunier d'Angibault* (1845), and *Le peche' de Monsieur Antoine* (1847). She was later accused of over-idealizing the peasants of her native Berry in her novels of country life, notably in *Jeanne* (1844), *La Mare au Diable* (1846), *La petite Fadette* (1849), *Francois le Champi* (1847), and *Les Matres Sonneurs* (1852). The criticism may have a basis, but the idealizations are so consistent that they reveal the reality behind the idealized figures. Of the so-called "romanesque" novels, the better known are *Jean de la Roche* (1860) and *Le Marquis de Villemer* (1861). George Sand wrote spontaneously, often without prearranged plan. In spite of this fault, her characters have a lifelike mobility which permits revealing development. In her descriptions of nature, accurate in detail and outline, her own personality is lyrically merged in the scene. V. Lucas translated and edited her *Letters* (1930), and M. J. Howe her *Intimate Journal* (1929).

26. RALPH WALDO EMERSON
1803-1882

Born in Boston, **Ralph Waldo Emerson** graduated from Harvard as class poet in 1821. In 1825 he returned to Cambridge to study divinity, though he felt no particular call to the ministry. As a young minister, Emerson met Ellen Louisa Tucker, the daughter of a Boston merchant. In 1829, soon after his election as the colleague-pastor of the Second Church of Boston, they were married. She died of tuberculosis only 17 months later. Through her death he inherited property which relieved him of financial worries, thus Emerson left the church to pursue his writing career

In 1832, he sailed for Europe, where he was to meet many prominent writers, of whom **Thomas Carlyle** became something of a mentor. They remained friends for over 40 years.

At home again, Emerson married Lydia Jackson of Plymouth. His first book, *Nature*, appeared in 1836, extolling infinite powers that would come to a person through nature if the spirit was awakened.

Ralph Waldo Emerson.

This book made a deep impression on select readers and on a small group of people who gathered in Emerson's study and elsewhere to discuss philosophical and religious problems. The neighbors nicknamed them as the "**Transcendental Club**," and the adjective became a label for the idealistic thinking of the period.

Emerson's *Essays* (1841) and *Essays: Second Series* (1844) applied his new thought to a wide variety of human concerns. These two books, together with his *Poems* (1847), established his reputation as a writer.

For the next 30 years Emerson continued to lecture throughout the Northeast. On the eve of the Civil War he published what is generally considered his most brilliantly written book, *The Conduct of Life* (1860). The final essay, "Illusions," is one of the most beautiful prose-poems that ever came from his pen. By this time, the transcendental hope of quickening a spiritual rebirth in the United States had faded.

Emerson's poem "Terminus," bidding himself to furl his sails, appeared in his second collection of poems, *May-Day and Other Pieces* (1867). The essays contained in *Society and Solitude* (1870) were all written before 1860. Meanwhile, Harvard bestowed on him an honorary degree and invited him to deliver a course of academic lectures there in 1871.

He made a third trip to Europe to carry out a cherished plan to see the Valley of the Nile. When he returned to Concord, the townspeople turned out to welcome him. Thereafter he sank more and more into serene forgetfulness until his death from pneumonia in April 1882. He was buried in Sleepy Hollow Cemetery.

Emerson was one of the last New Englanders to express the fiery energy of Puritan mysticism freed from the restraints of creed.

EDGAR ALLAN POE
1809-1849

The macabre and troubled genius who invented the horror genre in fiction, **Edgar Allan Poe** was born in Boston, the second son of Elizabeth Arnold, an English actress, and David Poe, a Baltimore law student who turned to acting and disappeared in 1810. Edgar was taken into the home of John and Frances Keeling Allan, a childless couple, by whom he was treated as a son, although he was never formally adopted. The tension between him and John Allan culminated in a violent quarrel, and in 1827, Poe left "home" and the next month turned up in Boston.

Poe's writing career can be said to have begun in earnest only after his expulsion from West Point in 1831. Needing money desperately, and realizing that poetry could not possibly support him, he turned to the writing of short stories for magazines such as **Nathaniel Parker Willis'** *Evening Mirror.* He finally achieved immense popular fame through the publication of "The Raven" (for which he received $10) on February 8, 1845.

Later he became editor, part owner, and for a short time, the owner of *The Broadway Journal.* He published *The Raven and Other Poems* in 1845. Despite these successes, Poe remained very poor. In 1846 he moved into a small cottage in Fordham, where he lived with his wife, who was now an invalid, and his mother-in-law. A year later, his wife Virginia died.

Poe published only one book after Virginia's death. *Eureka, a Prose Poem* (1848), contains Poe's most extended philosophical explanation of the universe, which he considered his magnum opus, but very few critics have agreed with him. They have generally preferred such short pieces as the strangely haunting "Ulalume" (1847) and the lyrical "Annabel Lee" (1849). He spent much time lecturing and giving public and private readings, which were somewhat in

Edgar Allan Poe.

the nature of poetry readings. He became a heavy drinker and his health deteriorated. Desperately in need of sympathy, he formed sentimental friendships with literary ladies, one of whom was Sarah Whitman, a Providence, Rhode Island poet, to whom he was briefly engaged.

A short time before his sudden and mysterious death in Baltimore, on October 7, 1849, he had courted and presumably considered himself engaged to Sarah Elmira Shelton, his boyhood "divinity," who was now a widow.

It is ironic that Poe should have named as his literary executor the Reverend **Rufus Wilmot Griswold.** Poe had often offended Griswold, a popular anthologist, by subjecting his literary tastes and abilities to scorching criticism. Poe's preoccupation with the macabre was an expression of a sensitive and brooding mind. He was able to create stories requiring for their solution a rigid process of mental deduction ("The Murders in the Rue Morgue," "The Purloined Letter") and stories of weird fantasy colored by ornate melancholy and subtle irrationality ("The Fall of the House of Usher," "Ligeria," "The Masque of the Red Death").

28. ALFRED TENNYSON
1809-1892

Alfred Tennyson was born in Somersby, a village in Lincolnshire, near the east coast of England, and took up poetry at Cambridge. During the early 1830s, there was a dearth of good poetry, so there was unusual critical interest in the works of younger poets such as **Elizabeth Barrett** and Tennyson. Tennyson's collections, the *Poems Chiefly Lyrical* of 1830 and the *Poems of 1832* (dated 1833), were exactingly reviewed. He published the two volumes of *Poems of 1842* with which critics and public alike were impressed. The grave blank verse and heroic mood of "Ulysses" and the brilliant word pictures and moral idealism of "Morte d'Arthur" pointed forward to the *Idylls of the King*.

On the death of **William Wordsworth** (see No.18), Tennyson was offered the poet laureateship. Tennyson wrote occasional poems on public events, the most notable being his *Ode on the Death of the Duke of Wellington* (1852). He dedicated the principal work of his later years, *Idylls of the King* to the memory of Prince Albert. He likened him to King Arthur and entered into an intimate friendship with his wife, Queen Victoria. Tennyson took a seat in the House of Lords as Baron Tennyson of Aldworth and Farrinford. From 1850 to the end, his private life was notably happy. In 1850 he married Emily Sellwood, the daughter of a lawyer in Lincolnshire, to whom he had first become engaged 13 years earlier. After the publication in 1855 of *Maud*, a long and passionate dramatic monologue, Tennyson turned to the Arthurian story. In 1859 he brought out *Idylls of the King*, four Arthurian narratives including "Enid" (later divided into "The Marriage of Geraint" and "Geraint and Enid"), "Vivien" (later "Merlin and Vivien"), "Elaine" (later "Lancelot and Elaine") and "Guinever." The success was extraordinary. In 1869 Tennyson added four more idylls in the volume *The Holy Grail and Other Poems* (including "The Holy Grail," "The Coming of Arthur," "Pelleas and Ettarre" and "The Passing of Arthur.") In his later years he wrote a number of poetic plays, many on themes from English history such as *Queen Mary* (1875), *Harold* (1876) , and *Becket* (1884).

In 1872, "Gareth and Lynette" and "The Last Tournament" (Tennyson's version of the story of Tristram and Isolde) were published. The last of the idylls, "Balin and Balan," appeared in 1885. Tennyson was neither a striking narrative poet nor a great creator of character, but the *Idylls* are rich in atmosphere, abundant in delicate pictures, and expressed in language of unsurpassed musical grace. Tennyson died at Aldworth in 1892 and is buried in Westminster Abbey. No English poet since his death has captured, as he did, the devotion of the general reader and the respect of the large majority of fair-minded critics.

Alfred Tennyson.

Born in Calcutta, **William Makepeace Thackeray** attended Trinity College, Cambridge, where he formed lifelong friendships with **Alfred Tennyson** (see No. 29) and **Edward FitzGerald**. Thackeray left Trinity College without earning a degree, and later joined *The National Standard*, a weekly newspaper. It failed, and Thackeray lost most of his inheritance which he had not already spent in gambling and living in the fast lane.

In 1842 he joined the staff of the recently founded humor magazine *Punch*. Most of his early writing was humorous or satiric, and was published under a variety of pen names. His first attempt at serious narrative, "A Shabby, Genteel Story," appeared in *Fraser's* in 1840, but was later used as the framework of *The Adventures of Philip* (1862). Among his *Punch* contributions were the prose parodies, collected as *Novels by Eminent Hands* (1856), and the sketches which formed *The Book of Snobs* (1847).

The publication of *Vanity Fair* in monthly parts, beginning in 1847, marked Thackeray's emergence as a major novelist. He followed it with the partly autobiographical *Pendennis* (1850), and with *Henry Esmond* (1852), and *The Newcomes* (1855). During these same years, he also wrote a number of separately published tales, satires, and Christmas stories, of which the most famous is *The Rose and the Ring* (1855).

In 1851, Thackeray delivered lectures on *The English Humorist of the Eighteenth Century*, which he repeated in the United States between November 1851 and April 1852. His tour was a great success. Socially, it won him a host of new friends, financially, it partly allayed his fear that he might leave his daughters in poverty. A second lecture series, on *The Four Georges*, was also given in America between November 1855 and April 1856. These American tours also furnished material for *The Virginians*

William Makepeace Thackeray.

(1859). In 1860 Thackeray became editor of *Cornhill Magazine*, to which he contributed *Lovel the Widower* and *The Roundabout Papers*. At his death on Christmas Eve in 1863, his novel *Denis Duval* was left unfinished.

Much of Thackeray's satiric attitude toward life was a defense mechanism to conceal basic sentimentality. Snobbish enough to be thrilled by favors from persons of title, he never quite got over feeling that it degraded a gentleman to write for a living. He loved his friends, and was loved by them, yet constantly got into hot water by foolish impulsive utterances and tactless personal allusions in his books.

As a result, a life darkened by tragedy was also spattered with the mud of silly squabbles. He ate and drank himself into a premature grave, but had written himself out before he died.

30. CHARLES DICKENS
1812-1870

One of the greatest, and certainly one of the most popular, English novelists, **Charles John Huffam Dickens** was born in Portsea, where his father, John Dickens, was a clerk. Charles was two years old when the family moved, first to London, and then to Chatham.

The sights, sounds, shapes, and colors of London, Rochester, and Chatham impressed the boy, shaped his sensibility and gave it the peculiar character which persevered throughout his life.

Dickens went to work as a reporter for such journals as *The True Sun, The Mirror of Parliament,* and *The Morning Chronicle.* His articles for these papers were characteristic in their defense of the pleasures of the common man. He showed himself to be a serious and responsible person even in those early days. He was a sharp critic of the senselessness of his family's way of life, and was obviously determined to make himself into a man of firm character. He was energetic and ambitious. He could be as hard as he could be jolly, he could be as angry as kind.

He had begun to write articles for *The Old Monthly Magazine* which were largely sketches of street scenes. Written to accompany illustrations by Cruikshank, and then Seymour, but later they were turned into fuller compositions and became the immortal *Pickwick Papers* (1837). This work was the beginning of Dickens' life as a popular author. His private life was complicated and, perhaps, deepened by a marriage that worked out its career under the pressures of boredom and misunderstanding.

Dickens' next book was *Oliver Twist* (1838), a deliberate contrast to *Pickwick Papers.* Dickens was enamored of variety, and he disliked repetition of method. *Oliver Twist* is an odd complex of realism and melodrama, and the tone is dark, fearsome and oppressive. While comedy had marked his first book, the young author exhibited the other side of his genius. He seemed, indeed, to write his literary signature at the outset of his career. His next book combined the qualities of the first two. *Nicholas Nickleby* (1839), is as melodramatic and dark as *Oliver Twist,* and as comic as *Pickwick Papers.* The mixture, however, is not always in solution, and the critic is severely tried in his attempt to find an organizing principle. Out of this book came the delightful and living characters Mr. Vincent Crummles, Miss Snevellicci, her astounding father, and Mr. Mantalini. Whatever the technical faults of the book, these characters survived for our pleasure.

As a result of his ambition to achieve universal appeal in his work, Dickens undertook the editorship of two magazines; *Household Words* and *All Year 'Round.*

Out of this experience, he conceived the scheme which was to be entitled *Master Humphrey's Clock* and was to consist of a series of stories told by a group of friends. This scheme, however, was not successful, in spite of the reintroduction of characters familiar to readers of his foregoing books. He immediately proceeded to write *Barnaby Rudge* (1840), which is remarkable for its adaptation of the romantic methods of **Sir Walter Scott** (see No. 19) and the descriptive scenes of the Gordon Riots.

Another book that grew out of the scheme of *Master Humphrey's Clock* was *The Old Curiosity Shop* (1841). This is perhaps the most sentimental and most popular of all Dickens' novels. Hundreds of people wrote to the author begging him not to let Little Nell die. This flattered Dickens and he was induced to prolong Little Nell's suffering beyond the limits of human endurance.

In January 1842, Dickens visited the United States, and wrote *American Notes* (1842), and *Martin Chizzlewit* (1844), as a

result. The latter book was twisted in plot to accommodate the American episodes, making it probably the most distorted novel in the language.

During 1844, Dickens began to show signs of nervous and physical fatigue. He had worked almost constantly, turning out novel after novel in addition to editorial responsibilities and family cares. He and his family moved to Genoa, Italy, where he produced *The Chimes* (1845), and continued a series of Christmas stories which had begun with *A Christmas Carol* in 1843. On his return to London, he became the first editor of *The Daily News*. He did not remain long, but returned to the continent, and at the end of this most restless period of his life finished a full-length novel, *Dombey and Son* (1848).

In 1849, a new and more fruitful vein was opened by the publication of *David Copperfield*. This is Dickens' masterpiece; rich, full, burdened with passion, sharp with memorable characterizations. It is Sentimental and melodramatic, yet moving in its presentation of a world that surpasses reality in that it is more lively than life, and always believable. It remains as a contribution of a great natural genius of letters.

The other books in this productive period were *Bleak House* (1853), a satire against the delays and idiocies of the law; *Hard Times* (1854), a novel of revolt which stated the position of the radical as opposed to errant individualism; *Little Dorrit* (1857), the successful and firmly formed historical novel; *A Tale of Two Cities* (1859), and *Great Expectations* (1861), which doubtless contains, in the first chapters at least, the finest of Dickens' writing.

Before his death, Dickens wrote one more full-length novel, *Our Mutual Friend* (1865), which is regarded by lovers of Dickens as one of his finest works; restrained, unified, and complete.

Charles Dickens.

In 1867, Dickens again traveled to the United States and there damaged his already weakened health by an extensive and energetic lecture tour. He had taken to reading from his own works, and the demands on him were many and insistent. On his return to England, he began work on a detective novel, *Edwin Drood*, in the style of his friend Wilkie Collins. In the midst of the work he died at the age of 58.

Dickens seemed to have little sense of emotional proportion. In his life as in his work, he was lavish. His activities included theatrical, social, and philanthropic undertakings.

At the height of his career, he was the shining literary light of his day. Crowds stood waiting impatiently for new installments of his novels. Although he was subjected to severe criticism in his lifetime for what seemed careless and often shoddy work, his fame did not diminish in force. He loved attention and popular acceptance.

31.32. CHARLOTTE BRONTE and EMILY BRONTE
1816-1855, 1818-1848

Charlotte, Emily and Anne were daughters of Patrick Bronte, an Irish-born Anglican clergyman, and Maria Branwell of Penzance in Cornwall. They were were born at Thornton, in the West Riding of Yorkshire, where their father was pastor. From an early age the girls and their brother Branwell wrote escapist romances about imaginary realms, some of which were posthumously published.

Charlotte and Emily went to school in Brussels in 1842. Emily stayed but a few months, Charlotte, however, returned for a second year. The personality and intellect of Constantin Heger, the husband of the headmistress, made a profound impression on her, and she fell in love with him. The sisters' plan for a girls' school faded, and they turned to writing. In 1846 they published *Poems of Currer, Ellis and Acton Bell*. Because of the discrimination faced by women writers at the time, they used these male pseudonyms (the initials corresponding with their own names) throughout their careers.

Historically, because women were discouraged from writing, much of what was available for them to read was by men.

Charlotte's first novel, *The Professor*, was rejected by a number of publishers, and appeared in print only after her death

She began her career with the resounding success of *Jane Eyre*, published in 1847. The realism and psychological insight in the representation of the governess heroines, based on Charlotte herself, and the brilliance in the descriptions of nature, the force and quickness of narrative, the startling incidents and surprising complications, make *Jane Eyre* one of the most interesting English novels ever.

In her next novel, *Shirley* (1849), she attempted something quite different, a real-

Charlotte Bronte.

istic panorama of Yorkshire life. It is an interesting document, but less well received critically than *Jane Eyre* and *Villette*, the last work that Charlotte lived to finish.

In *Villette* (1853) she poured out her excited responses to the many aspects of her life in Brussels, her contempt for Mme. Heger (who appears as Mme. Beck), her horror at Catholic morality and practices, her anger at worldly standards, and her passion for Heger (Paul Emanuel).

The heroine is almost another *Jane Eyre*, but drawn with the greater insight of full maturity. Paul Emanuel is the most interesting man in all her fiction, a portrait comparable to characters created by Fyodor Dostoevski (see No. 38).

There is some clumsiness in construction, and Charlotte's penchant for melodrama reappears. Still, if *Villette* was not as popular as *Jane Eyre*, it has a deeper tone, a richer atmosphere, and above all is surer in presenting the introspective tone.

In 1854 Charlotte married Arthur Bell Nicholls, who had been a clergyman at Haworth and returned to aid her father. Charlotte died in the following year, having already written two chapters of a promising fifth novel, to be called *Emma*.

Anne Bronte's two romance novels, *Alice Grey* (1847) and *The Tenant of Wildfell Hall* (1848), are not as highly regarded as the works of her sisters. The former is based on Anne's experiences as a governess, the latter on her horror at the spectacle of her brother's disintegration. Anne's books are are gracefully written and have an air of reality, but they do not produce the same exceptional impression. It has been suggested that they would not survive as widely read books without the reputation of Charlotte and Emily, and the interest in all that has to do with the Bronte family.

Emily was a true lyrical poet in a spiritual and mystical strain, and developed a style of austere intensity. Emily Bronte's only novel, *Wuthering Heights* (1847) was a masterpiece. Her death only a year later, cheated the world of major works which might have been.. The setting is a wild part of Yorkshire at the beginning of the century. The revenging character, Heathcliff (appropriately he has no Christian name), is a tragic figure who despite his cruel and brutal traits wins a measure of the reader's admiration.

His relationship with Catherine Earnshaw, whose will is as strong as his, has a mystical quality in which ordinary passion is quite lost. Their dialogue has a force and a simplicity that is unmatched in the fiction of the era. The conventionally good characters seem mediocre and slightly contemptible in contrast with the intensity of Catherine and Heathcliff.

The symbols of light and darkness in the characters are used with a subtlety and consistency which suggests an influence on **William Conrad** (see No. 50) and **James Joyce** (see No. 65).

A middle-aged housekeeper tells the story to a gentle young man from the south without really understanding the full importance of the incidents related. He adds to her story, but, despite his greater range of understanding, he falls short of grasping the essential meaning. These persons serve as the reader's representatives in the midst of a strange world and aid him in believing in the remarkable events and experiences which are the heart of Emily's subject.

Wuthering Heights is a monumental work of English literature. Though it has been widely praised, critics can not even begin to express the full essence of the novel. Not even Charlotte, who wrote the introduction to the second edition, could summarize the full breadth of its power.

Emily Bronte.

One of the first great American woman novelists, **Harriet Beecher** was born and grew up in Litchfield, Connecticut, where her father was a staunch supporter of Calvinistic orthodoxy.

At 14 she underwent the experience of religious conversion to strict, conservative Christianity. Being somewhat analytical in her reasoning, she remained deeply engrossed in theological issues throughout her life. Her earliest work, *The Mayflower*, appeared in 1843. Meanwhile, she had married her father's colleague, the Reverend **Calvin E. Stowe**, a learned and innocent-hearted man, and moved to Ohio, where she occasionally met a fugitive slave escaped from bondage.

Harriet Beecher Stowe returned to New England in 1850, just as the topic of the **Fugitive Slave Law** was the subject of heated discussion in the United States. Harriet conceived the idea of an old African-American dying under the lash but forgiving his persecutors, the germ and subsequent climax of *Uncle Tom's Cabin*. The novel, composed with intense emotion, was printed as a serial in *The National Era* in 1851-1852, and was immediately re-issued in book form. It proved to be an immense, if controversial, best-seller. In the United States north of the Mason-Dixon Line 300,000 copies were sold in a year. In England, where the work was pirated wholesale, the sale reached 1.5 million copies.

Harriet Beecher Stowe became an overnight sensation. When she visited England, she received an unprecedented ovation. To answer attacks on the accuracy of her novel, Harriet Beecher Stowe hastily compiled *A Key to Uncle Tom's Cabin* (1853), which was "not quite truthfully" advertised as containing the sources from which she had worked. A second antislavery novel, *Dred* (1856), undertook to show the evil effects of slavery on the plantation

Harriet Beecher Stowe.

owners. Neither of these books created the excitement that accompanied the publication of her first propaganda novel.

Though the crusade against slavery was growing in momentum, Harriet Beecher Stowe made no further contribution to the cause. Instead she revived her early interest in fiction dealing with everyday life in New England. *The Minister's Wooing* (1859), *The Pearl of Orr's Island* (1862), *Oldtown Folks* (1869), and *Poganuc People* (1878) placed her at the head of the school of New England realists. Though they never achieved best-seller status, these novels contain the most brilliant writing that Harriet Beecher Stowe ever accomplished.

During the last 30 years of her life she continued to write magazine and religious journal articles.

In the history of fiction, Stowe was a forerunner of the next generation of "local color" writers. But her chief claim to fame is her uncompromising work for human rights, and helping to end slavery.

Regarded as an American naturalist and philosopher, as well as an author, **Henry David Thoreau** was born in Concord, Massachusetts. He graduated from Harvard in 1837, and his writing career began in 1840, with the publication of an essay in *The Dial*, a newly founded transcendental magazine. **Transcendentalism** has been defined as "the recognition of the capacity of knowing truth intuitively, or of attaining knowledge transcending the reach of the senses."

From July 4, 1845 through September 6, 1847, Thoreau undertook a project destined to become his most famous. In his account of his stay at **Walden Pond**, Thoreau wrote how he "got back to nature." He cut his own timber for his shack, cut fire wood in the surrounding woods and most of his food he raised in his garden or picked in the woods.

"I am convinced," he wrote, "both by faith and experience, that to maintain oneself on this Earth is not a hardship but a pastime, if we will live simply and wisely. ... It is not necessary that a man should earn his living by the sweat of his brow, unless he sweats easier than I do."

During the stay at Walden, Thoreau wrote in journals the usual detailed account of his life and his thoughts. The book written at Walden, *A Week on the Concord and Merrimack Rivers*, was published that same year. *Walden*, an account of his experiment in living, published in 1854, was much more successful. Thoreau's chief contention was that men had become too enthusiastic about material comforts, about property, and about the nonessentials of civilization, and that therefore they were failing to live. His ideas are also elaborated upon in such works as *Excursions* (1863), *The Maine Woods* (1864), and *Cape Cod* (1865).

During his lifetime and, as a matter of fact, for a number of decades after his death, Thoreau did not have a very high reputation as a writer. In the 1920s, and again in the "counter-culture" period of the 1960s, he came to be recognized as a leading literary figure.

His philosophical and naturalistic works contributed to his growing reputation, but modern readers discovered interest in his social and political doctrines. His doctrine of simplicity as an antidote for the complexities of modern life proved attractive to many. Moreover, his ideas about government, most notably expressed in two essays, "Civil Disobedience" (1849) and "Life Without Principle" (1863) were influential, particularly in the British Labor Movement and in the passive resistance movement led by **Mohandas Gandhi** in India. "Civil Disobedience" was his best statement of his idea of rugged individualism.

Henry David Thoreau.

GEORGE ELIOT
1819-1880

Known by her pen name, **George Eliot**, **Mary Ann Evans** was born in a village in Warwickshire and attended school in Coventry. From 1851 to 1853 she was assistant editor of a local newspaper, *The Westminster Review* and formed close friendships with a number of distinguished writers and philosophers, notably **Herbert Spencer** and **George Henry Lewes**. She fell in love with Lewes and they lived happily together until Lewes' death in 1878; although Lewes remained married to his estranged first wife.

At the suggestion of Lewes she made her first attempt at fiction, and in 1856 produced a short story, "The Sad Fortunes of the Reverend Amos Barton," which was published in *Blackwood's Magazine* (1857). Her realistic tales of country life formed the collection *Scenes from Clerical Life* (1858), which made her one of the most important English writers of her time. However, because of discrimination against women writers, she wrote under the pseudonym "George Eliot."

Adam Bede (1859), her first novel, brilliantly displayed her talent for evoking background and atmosphere, and won her an even wider audience. In 1860, she published the autobiographical *Mill on the Floss*, a revealing analysis of a child's emotions and reactions. It was followed by *Silas Marner* (1861), a story of a country miser. In 1861 she visited Italy in search of a theme for a historical novel. The result was *Romola* (1863). It was her longest and most complex work, but lacked the charm of her earlier fiction. *Felix Holt, the Radical* (1866) was a melodramatic story of a young political reformer. Poetry in this book prepared her readers for *The Spanish Gypsy* (1868), a laborious effort in verse which enjoyed popularity though it never approached true poetry.

Her last works were *Middlemarch* (1871-1872), in which she returned to the study of provincial manners, *Daniel Deronda* (1876), a fictionalized view of Zionism, and *Impressions of Theophrasts's Such* (1879), was a collection of short stories. After Lewes' death she edited some of his unpublished work and established the George Lewes Scholarship to aid students engaged in scientific work. In May 1880, she married John Walter Cross, an intimate friend of both Lewes and herself, but she died in December of the same year.

Mary Ann (George Eliot) Evans.

36. WALT WHITMAN
1819-1892

Considered by some to be the greatest American poet of the nineteenth century, **Walt Whitman** was born in West Hills, Long Island. His temperance novel *Franklin Evans; or The Inebriate* was published in the magazine *The New World*, (1842), and he also published a number of sentimental poems.

In 1848, Whitman became editor of an antislavery newspaper, *The Freeman*, and between 1850 and 1854, he supported himself by working for several newspapers, contributing to various periodicals, and, in partnership with his father, building and selling houses.

In 1855, Whitman published the first collection of his new poetry in free verse, *Leaves of Grass*. It was an extraordinary publication, and is considered one of the most interesting first editions in American literature. His thoughts were influenced by that of the Quakers and of the French and American romanticists, particularly **Ralph Waldo Emerson** (see No. 26). "I was simmering, simmering," wrote Whitman. "Emerson brought me to a boil."

Whitman refused, as a rule, to employ regular rhythms. Although his poem in conventional meter, "O Captain! My Captain !" is his most popular. His verse is not rhymed, and the line lengths are not metrical units, but units corresponding to the cadences of oral delivery.

Between 1857 and 1859, Whitman was an editor of *The Brooklyn Daily Times*. When the Civil War began, Whitman became a volunteer nurse in Washington, supporting himself by reporting for various newspapers and by working part time in an army paymaster's office. After the war, he worked in the attorney general's office.

Drum Taps, based on his war experiences, was published in 1865. Although he was never in actual combat, some scholars have called him, with some justification, "a

Walt Whitman.

war-born poet" because he drew so much from the soldiers he met.

The 1860s saw the beginning of a growing recognition of Whitman. The year 1871 saw the publication not only of the fifth regular edition of *Leaves of Grass,* but also of *Democratic Vistas*, a book about post-Civil War America. On February 22, 1873, in Washington, Whitman suffered a stroke and went to live with his brother George in Camden. Partially recovered, he spent several summers on a nearby farm and traveled extensively in the East, the Far West (1879) and in Canada (1880). He published *Specimen Days* and *Collect* (1882) and *November Boughs* (1888). In 1888, another stroke confined him to a wheelchair, but he continued to write and to visit with the many admirers who traveled to Camden.

Born in New York City, **Herman Melville** worked as a cabin boy on the *Highlander*, a merchant vessel bound for Liverpool at age 18. His later book, *Redburn* (1849) offered an account of his first voyage to Liverpool, and his first impressions of the life of a sailor and of his observations of English life. After his return in 1840, he taught school in Massachusetts, and made his first attempts at writing. Soon, however, he decided to sail again, bound for the Pacific.

In July 1842 he and a shipmate deserted the *Acushnet* in the Marquesas Islands, where they lived for several weeks among the **Typees** (cannibals). Melville escaped aboard a whaler, and spent the next several years at sea, including a year with the US Navy. As a writer, his work flowed from his own interesting and unusual experiences, and the maritime stories he heard as a child and during his years as a sailor, where he'd swapped yarns with many shipmates.

Typee (1846) told of his life among the cannibals and of what he had learned concerning their customs and way of living. His books detailed his maturing view of life through his experiences at sea. *Ornoo* (1847) told of his subsequent stay in Tahiti and the nearby islands, and offered pictures of life at sea and among the natives, while *White Jacket* (1850) was based on his service with the US Navy.

The first two books were highly successful in attracting the interest of the reading public, because of the novelty of their materials, their workmanlike style, their frankness about sex and their sensational attacks on what was being done to the native people by missionaries on the islands.

Melville's masterpiece, *Moby Dick* (1851), recounted a whaling voyage under the leadership of Captain Ahab, who was obsessed with a desire to hunt down the great white whale, **Moby Dick**. By the time the philosophical and allegorical narrative tells of the long pursuit of this "monster" and of the whale's final triumph, Melville has covered thoroughly the topic of whales and whalers. Free will and predestination, man's pursuit of elusive truth, and the nature of evil and knowledge are some of the important themes in *Moby Dick*.

Later work (1852-1856) included *Pierre*, a historical novel, *Israel Potter*, *Piazza Tales*, a collection of short stories, and in 1856, *The Confidence Man*, a satirical novel. At the time of his death he left unpublished his last long work of fiction, *Billy Budd*. This masterly novelette was not printed until 1924, when a new generation had rediscovered Melville and had begun to give him overdue recognition as a great writer of philosophical fiction.

Herman Melville.

The great Russian novelist **Fyodor Mikhailovich Dostoevski** was born in Moscow and studied military engineering, but turned to writing because of his need to express his thoughts on social injustice. His first work, *Poor Folk*, a short novel in letters, appeared in 1846 and brought him instant fame. Within the next three years, he wrote nearly a dozen remarkable short stories, of which the most notable is *The Double*, a penetrating psychological study.

Dostoevski's early writings are marked by a preoccupation with and pity for "the little man," the victim of an oppressive social system. His later writings are significant for the insights they offer into Russian culture and into the workings of the human mind generally. Tense with passionate drama, built on complex plots in which crime plays a prominent part, his sprawling novels derive much of their interest from their incorporation of his ideas about ethics.

He was at work on a full-sized novel when, early in May 1849, he was arrested and subsequently brought to trial on the charge of having been involved in a subversive organization. Dostoevski was sentenced to four years hard labor in Siberia, and while there, he married the widow of a minor Siberian official.

When the couple were allowed to return to the capital, he took up his pen again, writing fiction and working for two short-lived monthlies, published by his brother and edited by himself. They published his novel, *The Insulted and Injured* (1861), his disguised prison reminiscences; *The House of the Dead* (1862); and two powerful tales, *An Unpleasant Predicament* (1862) and *Note From the Underground* (1864). These works helped establish his importance as a novelist, and he even toured Western Europe.

His wife died in 1864, and the magazine that was under Dostoevski's management

Fyodor (Feodor) Mikhailovich Dostoevski.

failed. He assumed all the debts incurred and also undertook to support his deceased brother's family and his own stepson. In 1867, he married the stenographer whom he had employed in order to meet a deadline.

In 1866, he published two novels, *The Gambler* and *Crime and Punishment*. The latter was the first of the great works of fiction that earned him a worldwide reputation. While he was out of Russia, he wrote *The Idiot* (1868) and *The Eternal Husband* (1870) and began *The Possessed*. Back in St. Petersburg, he completed this tale, which attacked the embryonic Russian revolutionary movement. He also composed the novels *A Raw Youth* (1875) and *The Brothers Karamazov* (1879-1880), his crowning achievement.

In his last years he took time off from the writing of fiction to start work on his memoirs. He commented on current events and his opinions on a wide variety of topics, including the virtues of Russian folklore and Russia's messianic destiny. He contributed these to a conservative weekly which he edited in 1873.

The father of modern science fiction, **Jules Verne** was born in Nantes, studied law in Paris, and wrote for the stage before he began contributing science fiction to the *Magazine d'Education*. His enormously successful *Five Weeks in a Balloon* (1863) was the first of a long series of imaginative tales which exploited popular interest in the actual and potential achievements of nineteenth century science.

His success continued with *A Journey to the Center of the Earth* in 1864 and *Twenty Thousand Leagues Under the Sea* in 1870. The latter of which featured the legendary arch-villain **Captain Nemo**, skipper of the enormous submarine *Nautilus*. His smooth, fast-paced writing style and his detailed descriptive passages truly anticipate the style of twentieth century science fiction. Riding the crest of public interest in science and invention in the nineteenth century, Verne's books became immensely popular.

Not only were they well-paced adventure stories, but they also transported readers to places they had never been. Verne focused the action of his novels in yet unexplored locations like outer space, the bottom of the ocean and deep inside the Earth, but in novels such as *The Children of Captain Grant* (1868), he carried his readers to South America and Australia, lands that were just as remote and exotic for most Europeans as the moon.

He sought to convey mystery by setting his works in places which were unfamiliar, yet believable and realistic. *The Mysterious Island* (1875) was set on the same, while *Captain Hatteras* (1866) and *The Sphinx of Ice* (1897) took place at the poles.

Readers also loved Verne's books because they had thrilling, fast-paced plots. In the immortal classic *Around the World in Eighty Days* (1873), the engaging hero **Phineas Fogg** is constantly in motion, never pausing for more than a couple of days in any one place, because he is taking part in the race of his lifetime.

Verne was as hard-working and prolific a writer as he was successful. Between 1878 and 1880 he published four novels, as well as a three-volume history of exploration entitled *The Discovery of the Earth*. In his later years, he indulged his continuing passion for invention with *Clipper of the Clouds* (1886), in which he imagined fleets of gargantuan airships populating the sky—an idea that not only accurately foreshadowed the era of the *Hindenberg* and other airships of the 1930s, but also the jumbo jets that appeared in the 1970s. He also created worlds that are still yet to be, such as in his novel *The Day of An American Journalist in 2889 AD*.

He had an amazing insight into the trend of scientific invention, and many of his imaginary creations, from the submarine to the fax machine, were actually invented.

Jules Verne.

40. LEO NIKOLAEVICH TOLSTOY
1828-1910

The great Russian writer and moralist **Leo Nikolaevich Tolstoy**, was born in Yasnaya Polyana. At the age of 23, he enlisted in the Tsar's army, and while his unit was stationed in the Caucasus, he wrote part of a semi-autobiographical tale, *Childhood, Boyhood and Youth,* which was published in 1852.

After his military service, which included the Crimean War, Tolstoy continued to write. He produced several popular novelettes and short stories, notably *Two Hussars* (1856), *Three Deaths* (1859) and *Polikushka* (1860).

He was keenly interested in education, and conducted classes for peasant children at Yasnaya Polyana on the principle that instruction must be completely free from discipline and compulsion. Years later, when he was already a famous novelist, he compiled a primer, an arithmetic book, and a graded reader, which were widely used in the primary schools.

At the age of 34 Tolstoy married the 18-year-old daughter of a Moscow physician and settled down at Yasnaya Polyana to the life of a gentleman farmer, who was an author as well. In 1863, he published *The Cossacks*, a novel inspired by his military service, on which he had been at work sporadically for nearly a dozen years. He also completed *War and Peace*, a monumental chronicle of Russian life as the nobility knew it during the Napoleonic wars. It was inspired by his interest in the injustice of class distinctions that was very prevalent in Russia.

Another great serial work, *Anna Karenina,* which appeared in 1875-1877, was a novel of adultery and of married happiness in an aristocratic setting; a story that combined realism with a message about morality among the upper classes.

This book, along with *War and Peace*, earned Tolstoy worldwide fame as a writer,

Leo Nikolaevich Tolstoy.

and rank with the greatest fiction ever written.

Tolstoy's work is influenced by his adopting a form of Christianity free from dogma and ritual and based on kindness. His faith led him to denounce both the traditional church and government. He supported radical causes, but he disapproved of violence, war, capital punishment and eating meat.

Tolstoy did not give up fiction writing. He turned out novelettes, notably *The Death of Ivan Ilyich* (1886), *Master and Man* (1893) and the novel *Resurrection* (1899). He questioned the value of science and of the achievements of the industrial revolution. In 1888 he signed over his possessions to his family, and three years later he placed those of his works written after 1881 in the public domain, judiciously deciding to keep his rights to *War and Peace* and *Anna Karenina*.

On November 10, 1910, after a fight with his wife, Tolstoy wandered away from home and was found dead in a lonely railway station ten days later.

41. EMILY ELIZABETH DICKINSON
1830-1886

The daughter of a prominent lawyer, **Emily Elizabeth Dickinson** was born in Amherst, Massachusetts, where she spent nearly her entire life. She attended Amherst Academy and spent one year at Mary Lyon's Female Seminary in South Hadley, now Mount Holyoke College. An extremely shy and introspective person, she remained quietly at home and did not travel, from the time she was 19 until her death. After she was 30 she withdrew more and more from casual contact with the world in order to concentrate on her writing.

Emily Dickinson's work is remarkable for its defiance of Victorian convention, for its absolute honesty, its intensity and for the way that the author displayed such reverence for intrinsic values.

Her artistic technique minimizes smoothness, especially its disregard for niceties of rhyme and places full emphasis on substance.

Because of her shyness, she did not circulate her work widely, and only a handful of her poems were published during her lifetime.

After her death, hundreds of her lyrical jewels were discovered and brought to life in the pages of posthumous works. Many were finished and studiously copied, while others were clearly not yet where the author wanted to take them. The first collection of Emily Dickinson's work was published in 1890, but the third was not issued until 1945.

Her poems speak of great renunciation and hint that the "atom" she preferred was an unnamed married man, but this attachment seems to have been more a matter of introverted devotion than outgoing passion.

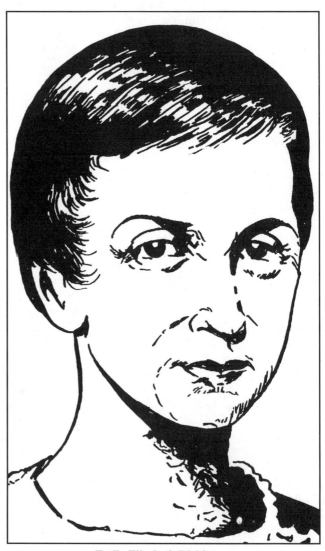

Emily Elizabeth Dickinson.

The author of *Little Women*, one of the most enduring novels for young people in American literature, **Louisa May Alcott** was born in Germantown, Pennsylvania, and was raised in Boston and Concord, Massachusetts.

She was educated mainly by her father, **Amos Bronson Alcott**, who compelled his family to work to support his ultimately unsuccessful cooperative commune near Boston, which was called "Fruitlands." She wrote of this experimental lifestyle in her short account "Transcendental Wild Oats." Her impressions of Fruitlands probably influenced her later work as well. While *Little Women* is set in a traditional home (albeit with the father away at war), *Little Men* is set in a communal boarding school.

Louisa tried teaching, sewing, and working as a household servant, and considered acting and play writing before she found her true calling. Her first success was with stories and poems in the *Atlantic Monthly*.

During the Civil War, she served as a nurse until her health deteriorated. Her impressions of the war, originally written as her letters to her family, were published as *Hospital Sketches* (1863), and became extremely popular with readers, and enjoyed great success.

The central characters of her most famous book, *Little Women* (1867), were based on Louisa and her sisters. The bright, outgoing and ambitious character Jo, was Louisa's own version of herself. The immense popular success led to the publication of a continuation in a second volume with the same title. *Little Men* (1871) featured Jo as an adult, was even more successful, and from then on the family's fortunes were secure.

She continued writing until two years before her death, when *Jo's Boys* was published. She was known for her cheerful, sturdy, energetic characters, and for her realistic American scenes.

Louisa May Alcott.

43. LEWIS CARROLL
1832-1898

The Reverend **Charles Lutwidge Dodgson** was an English cleric and mathematician who authored books for children under the pen name **Lewis Carroll**. Dodgson was born in Daresbury, Cheshire, where his father, the Reverend Charles Dodgson, was vicar. After attending Rugby School, young Dodgson attended Christ Church College, at Oxford, where he received his degree in 1854. The following year, he was appointed lecturer in mathematics at Christ Church, a post which he continued to hold until his retirement in 1881. In 1861 he was ordained deacon in the Church of England.

Lewis Carroll was a prim, celibate clergyman, frequently ill at ease in the company of adults. He displayed the most attractive side of his nature to a long succession of little girls. He entertained them with many stories besides the ones which got written down, to whom he wrote charming letters, and for whom he devised innumerable conundrums and mathematical games. Because of this attention to young girls,

Dodgson's intentions have occasionally been called into suspicion as dishonorable.

Dodgson took the name Lewis Carroll from Carolus Ludovicus, a Latinized version of "Charles Lutwidge," in 1865, when he published *Alice's Adventures in Wonderland*. This story was originally written for the entertainment of **Alice Liddell** (later Mrs. Reginald Hargreaves), young daughter of Dodgson's friend Henry George Liddell, Greek lexicographer and dean of Christ Church. The manuscript of the original version, illustrated by Lewis Carroll himself, is now in the Widener Library at Harvard University.

In the published version and its sequel, *Through the Looking Glass* (1871), the illustrations were by Sir John Tenniel of *Punch Magazine*. Tenniel's pictures have become so much a part of the text that later attempts to supplant them, even in the 1951 Walt Disney film, pale by comparison.

In 1876, Lewis Carroll published *The Hunting of the Snark*, and in 1883 a collection of nonsense verse called *Rhyme? and Reason?* His last attempt at a child's story was *Sylvie and Bruno* (Part I, 1889, Part II, 1893).

While "Lewis Carroll" wrote fantasies with strange, imaginary worlds, Dodgson published a number of mathematical treatises under his own name. *Euclid and his Modern Rivals* (1879) is usually spoken of as the most valuable to students of the history of mathematical theory. This curious "double life" has interested biographers ever since.

In his two classic books, Dodgson, as Carroll, achieved a sort of logical nonsense which has made Alice as great a favorite with grownups as it has always been with the children for whom it was written.

Charles Lutwidge (Lewis Carroll) Dodgson.

44. BRET HARTE
1836-1902

A contemporary of **Samuel Clemens** (see No.45), **Francis Brette "Bret" Harte**, crossed the former's path in Calaveras County, California; a fact that is still celebrated locally.

Harte was a short story writer, poet and novelist, born in Albany, New York, the son of a school teacher. He had little formal education, but read widely in his father's library. His favorite author was Dickens, whose influence can be seen in Harte's character development, as well as his writings. In 1854 he moved to California, where he worked as an druggist's helper, tutor, school teacher, express messenger, miner, and printer's devil. In 1860 he settled in San Francisco, working as a compositor on *The Golden Era*, a newspaper to which he had already contributed a quantity of fugitive verse and prose.

From 1863 to 1867 he was secretary of the Branch Mint and served for a time as editor of *The Californian*. His contributions to the *Golden Era* and *The Californian*, collected in book form as *The Lost Galleon* (1867) and *Condensed Novels* (1867), won him a local reputation. He first received wide recognition in 1868 for stories that reflected his considerable knowledge of the American West which appeared in print after he became editor of a California magazine, *The Overland Monthly*.

His short stories, "The Luck of Roaring Camp" and "The Outcasts of Poker Flat," were published as Dickensian portraits of the last frontier. His whimsy and eye for local color proved irresistible to the American reading public, and when he left California in 1870 he was quite famous.

At the same time, he won further fame as a humorist with "Plain Language from Truthful James" which introduced readers

Bret Harte.

to the stoic Mid-westerner who became a stock figure in American literature. Harte's best short stories were collected as *Luck of Roaring Camp* and *Tales of the Argonauts* (1875). His work was particularly characterized by a deep understanding of life in the West and the personalities of the people he'd met in the mountains and mining camps of California and other states.

In 1878 he left his wife and children and went to Europe, where he served as United States consul in Prussia and Glasgow. He finally settled in London in 1885, where he resumed writing, working with his familiar California frontier themes. His later work was popular in England because of a fascination with for Western Americana, but in America, his reworking of early material made him less popular.

45. MARK TWAIN (SAMUEL CLEMENS)
1835-1910

More often than not, **Samuel Langhorne Clemens** is cited as being the greatest American writer of the nineteenth century. Under the pen name **Mark Twain**, Clemens is the author of enduring classics that helped define American literature. Clemens was born in Florida, Missouri and grew up in Hannibal, Missouri, which was a little frontier town of less than 500. He was influenced by life on the Mississippi River and the name "Mark Twain" was derived from a term used by boatmen sounding the depth of the river.

In 1847 the death of his father ended the boy's schooling, and young Sam became a printer's apprentice. He learned to be a writer by working as a typesetter and reading various books which interested him.

His earliest writings were skits for his brother Orion's Hannibal newspaper. A sketch, "The Dandy Frightening the Squatter," published in *The Carpet Bag* (Boston) in 1852, his first published story, was a tale of life on the Mississippi River. Between 1853 and 1857, as a journeyman printer, Clemens worked in St. Louis, New York, Philadelphia, Muscatine, Keokuk, and Cincinnati. A letter written to a sweetheart while he worked in Keokuk showed, more clearly than anything else he wrote in this period, his skill in inventing imaginative humor. A series of sketches, "The Snodgrass Letters," signed with the pseudonym **Thomas Jefferson Snodgrass**, were published in the *Keokuk Post* in 1856 and 1857. These showed that Clemens, like many another humorist of the 1850s, was fond of using misspellings, puns and weirdly fashioned sentences for humorous effects.

The letters were written during a trip down the Mississippi River. Recalling his boyhood memories of the glamour of river life, he arranged to become a pilot's apprentice, won his license in due time, and then served as a pilot until the Civil War interrupted river traffic. While a steamboat man, he furthered his literary development at intervals by writing skits for various newspapers. He served briefly in the Confederate Army, and then went overland to Carson City, Nevada with his brother Orion, who had a job in the territorial government.

In Nevada, Clemens was caught up in the fever of the mining country, and his letters home were full of accounts of investments and prospecting trips. When, however, none of his ventures panned out well, he became a reporter on *The Virginia City Territorial Enterprise* in 1862.

It was while working on this paper in the teeming and colorful Washoe district that he really found himself as a humorist. He entered into his career as a professional writer and realized that his sporadic journalistic activities had been no more than the amateurish exercises preparing him for real achievements. In 1863, while reporting on meetings of the Nevada legislature, he first used the pseudonym Mark Twain. In 1864, he went to San Francisco, where he worked for several newspapers developing his humorous style and his wry sense of irony.

A few of his sketches were reprinted in Eastern publications. One Story, "Jim Smiley and His Jumping Frog," published in *The New York Saturday Press*, Nov. 18, 1865, was a national sensation. The story was about a jumping frog race in which the favorite is secretly fed buckshot by the owner of a rival frog.

The next year a trip to the Sandwich Islands (now Hawaii) produced not only a series of humorous travel letters to *The Sacramento Union,* but also a serious article published in *Harper's Magazine.*

In 1866, Twain became a correspondent for *The Alta California.* One series that he wrote for that paper told the details of a journey eastward by boat, and of his visits to New York and the Middle West in 1867.

The year 1867 saw the publication of Mark Twain's first book, *The Celebrated Frog of Calaveras County.* A collection of sketches, it saw, too, his first appearance as a humorous lecturer on an Eastern platform.

The year was also notable for his trip to the Holy Land with an excursion party, duly recorded in letters published in *The Alta California* and *The New York Tribune.* These letters, collected and revised, were published as *Innocents Abroad* (1869), a book based on his experiences travelling in Europe, which secured his fame as a humorist. A year later, he married **Olivia Langdon** of Elmira, NY.

Mark Twain.

Clemens became part owner of *The Buffalo Express* in 1869, and served for a time as a newspaper editor in Buffalo and a column conductor in *The Galaxy.* Soon he severed his connections with the newspaper and the magazine, moved to Hartford, and became exclusively a lecturer and author. A number of books reaped handsome royalties, notably *Roughing It* (1872), based on his far western experiences, and *The Gilded Age* (1873), written in collaboration with Charles Dudley Warner as an expose of the speculative and corrupt spirit of the period.

His best known and most remembered works began to appear late in the 1870s. *The Adventures of Tom Sawyer* (1876), *Life on the Mississippi* (1883) and *The Adventures of Huckleberry Finn* (1884), which told of Hannibal and the river life he had known in youth, were well received milestones of his career.

Also of note were *The Prince and the Pauper* (1882) and *A Connecticut Yankee in King Arthur's Court* (1889), the former of which dealt seriously and the latter humor-ously with historical materials. Despite the remarkable financial success of these books, he found himself bankrupt in 1894. He had lived on a lavish scale and had made a number of disastrous investments, particularly in the development of a linotype machine and in the Charles L. Webster Publishing Company.

Though officially declared insolvent, Clemens promised to pay his creditors dollar for dollar. A lecture tour around the world and the publication of two books, *Personal Recollections of Joan of Arc* (1896) and *Following the Equator* (1897), helped make possible the fulfillment of his promise.

His bankruptcy, however, and the death of his daughter Susan in 1896 and of his wife in 1904, turned Clemens' mood to deep pessimism. Threads of this could be found is his works as early as the 1880s, but after the turn of the century, he grew increasingly bitter with the passing years, and published no new works.

The great English novelist and poet **Thomas Hardy** was born in Upper Bockhampton in Dorset. Although he was apprenticed to an architect at 16, and made a reasonably good living in this profession until he was in his middle thirties, Hardy was not enthusiastic about his work and prepared himself for a literary career while still in his teens. Consistent rejection of his poetry led him to try fiction writing, but his first novel, an ironic social commentary, *The Poor Man and the Lady* (part of which was posthumously published as *An Indiscretion in the Life of on Heiress*), was considered too "socialistic" for publication. His second try, *Desperate Remedies* (1871), a novel in the manner of the Wilkie Collins thriller, was printed.

It was not until the publication of *Far from the Madding Crowd* in 1874 that he felt secure enough to marry Emma Lavinia Gifford and give up architecture. During the next 21 years, he devoted himself to the series of novels that have since become known as the "Wessex Novels" because of their usual setting in the region that went by that name in King Alfred's time. Despite the geographical limitation of scene, these novels were generally more universal than the typical work of Victorian novelists because of Hardy's candid presentation of non-sentimental human behavior. He always viewed his characters as exemplars of universal natural laws.

After *Jude the Obscure* (1895) was severely attacked for its frank treatment of sex and marriage, Hardy decided to devote himself entirely to poetry, where he believed he could speak out to a more discriminating audience. However, up until the last years of his life when he became "the grand old man of English literature,"

he was subjected to periodic attacks of what his readers regarded as his pessimistic fatalism.

In commenting on society at large, Hardy believed that the world was "slowly improving" although some readers and critics felt that he overemphasized the somber. Such novels as *Far from the Madding Crowd* (1874), *The Return of the Native* (1878), *The Mayor of Casterbridge* (1885), *Tess of the D'Urbervilles* (1891), and the once infamous, now famous, *Jude the Obscure* seem securely entrenched against quick oblivion by the praise of competent critics. Hardy's genius, as revealed in each of these, is his power of depicting nature as a symbolic background for his characters and as an organic part of the action of the story.

It is probable, however, that Hardy will be remembered longest for his philosophical epic, *The Dynasts* (1904-1908).

Thomas Hardy.

The great popular Scottish novelist of the late nineteenth century, **Robert Louis Balfour Stevenson** was born in Edinburgh. From infancy, Stevenson was confined to his bed much of the time by tuberculosis and a myriad of other illnesses. The experience formed the basis for "The Land of Counterpane" and other stories of childhood illness in his *A Child's Garden of Verses* (1885).

During the 1870s, Stevenson contributed numerous articles and stories to magazines. His first book was *An Inland Voyage* (1878), the record of a canoe trip through France which he took with his friend Sir Walter Simpson. A camping tour in the Cevennes in 1878 furnished the material for *Travels With a Donkey* (1879).

While in France, Stevenson fell deeply in love with Fanny Osborne, an American woman, and followed her back to the States, a trip he recorded in his stories "The Amateur Emigrant" and "Across the Plains." In San Francisco and Monterey he tried to support himself entirely by his pen, though a recurrence of tuberculosis made the effort difficult.

In 1880, he finally married Fanny and they moved to Calistoga, famed for its mineral baths and alleged healthful environment. This stint is described in his *The Silverado Squatters* (1883).

They later returned to Europe, where Stevenson's first popular success in fiction came in 1882, with *Treasure Island*, a story a young cabin boy on a treasure-seeking ship that is taken over by pirates in the Caribbean.

While *Treasure Island* was popular with children as well as adults, *The Strange Case of Dr. Jekyll and Mr. Hyde* (1886) and *Kidnapped* (1886) and *The Master of Ballantrae* (1889) established his reputation among older readers because of their stronger, more mature symbolism.

Robert Louis Stevenson.

In 1887, Stevenson returned to the United States, and spent a winter at Saranac Lake under the care of Dr. Trudeau, the famous pioneer in the treatment of tuberculosis. His health mended sufficiently for him to undertake a long series of voyages in the South Seas. In 1889 he finally settled down at Vailima, Samoa, where he lived until he died of a cerebral hemorrhage in 1894. Here, he enjoyed the best creative period of his life. Besides such brilliant short stories as "The Bottle Imp" and "The Beach of Falesli," he completed during these years the sequel to *Kidnapped*, published in England as *Catriona* (1893) and in the United States as *David Balfour, The Wrecker* (1892) and *The Ebb Tide* (1894).

The latter two were written in collaboration with his stepson Lloyd Osbourne, perhaps partly with a view to protecting their American copyright. *Weir of Hermiston* (1897) and *St. Ives* (1898) were left unfinished at his death but the latter was published with the concluding chapters supplied by **A.T. Quiller-Couch.**

Born in Dublin in 1856, the flamboyant Irish dramatist and poet **Oscar Fingal O'Flahertie Wills Wilde**, lived life in the words of his catch-phrase "Nothing exceeds like excess."

Wilde's plays are, with the exception of the last, a curious mixture of brilliant dramatic invention and hackneyed imitation of the well-made problem comedies, which were the dramatic staple of his period. They are seen by historians as being, in their intentions, similarly a mixture of brilliantly witty, fundamentally serious skirmishes against stupid conventionality and stereotyped sentimental themes. The mixture is characteristic of Wilde's whole career. At his brilliant best, as in *The Importance of Being Earnest*, he produced an irrepressibly humorous and formidably shrewd commentary on the society of his time.

Wilde's mother was a writer and had a literary salon in Dublin, so young Oscar was brought up in a world of wit. The charismatic Wilde quickly became a public figure, a sort of professional celebrity. As such, he was known nationally and became a subject for caricature in the humor magazine *Punch* and in Gilbert and Sullivan's operetta *Patience*.

His most intensive literary period began in 1888 with publication of *The Happy Prince and Other Tales* (1888), and was followed by *The Picture of Dorian Gray* (1891), an imitation of Huysmans' *A Rebours*. He followed this with a volume of essays and began his short but very brilliant career as a dramatist. His first comedy, *Lady Windermere's Fan*, was produced in 1892. In 1893, he was refused a license to produce his play *Salome* in London because of its suggestive content. Written in French, *Salome* was published in France and produced in Paris by Sarah Bernhardt in 1896. It was translated into English by Lord Alfred Douglas in 1894.

An Ideal Husband and *The Importance of Being Earnest* were both produced in 1895, and were both playing when Wilde, as if courting disaster, sued the Marquis of Queensbury for criminal libel. He lost and was immediately brought to trial and convicted for offenses under the Criminal Law Amendment Act. He spent two years at hard labor and was ruined financially as well as in reputation by his libelous indiscretions.

After his release from jail he lived in France. The single literary product of this period was the sincere but excessively rhetorical *Ballad of Reading Goal* (1898).

Oscar Wilde.

Few films are included in more "ten best" lists than the legendary *Wizard of Oz*. Though it was released in 1939, it continues to be an enduring classic.

Why is it so popular? Almost certainly, its lasting impact on American iconography is a result of its carefully crafted imaginary universe and its magical, yet deeply philosophical, characters. Yet it is only the tip of an amazing series of tales of the mythical **Oz** that spilled forth from the creative genius of **Lyman Frank Baum**.

The creator of the land called Oz, L. Frank Baum was born in Chittenango, New York and educated in Syracuse. He entered the newspaper field in 1880, and edited papers in Aberdeen, South Dakota from 1888 to 1890, and in Chicago from 1897 to 1902.

His legendary series of "Oz" books were staple juvenile fiction for many years and were continued by other writers after Baum's death. The first of the series, *The Wonderful Wizard of Oz* (1900), was followed by *The New Wizard of Oz* (1903), *The Land of Oz* (1904), *Ozma of Oz* (1907), and other fantasies.

Lyman Frank Baum.

Among Baum's other books, all of which had similar themes, were *Mother Goose in Prose* (1897-1902), *Father Goose: His Book* (1899), *The Life and Adventures of Santa Claus* (1902), *Baum's Fairy Tales* (1908), and a number of lesser known works, published under the pen names "Edith Van Dyne," "Schuyler Stanton," and "Floyd Akers."

He wrote sequels for most of these stories, which had sequels and were very popular at the time, though they have largely been overshadowed by the initial work. Before the 1939 classic film with **Judy Garland** as Dorothy, *The Wizard of Oz* was also popular as a musical extravaganza in 1901, starring the comedian Fred Stone as the Scarecrow, his first successful role.

1857-1924

Born in Poland in 1857, **Teodor Josef Konrad Korzeniowski** was the son of a Polish patriot and writer who was exiled in Russia and died when his son was 13. The boy had a desire, incomprehensible to his relatives, for a life at sea. Brought up in a country with only a minimal seacoast and knowing English only through the translations made by his father, he was nevertheless determined to be an English seaman. In 1874 he went to sea from Marseilles, and after four years in French ships, he sailed as an ordinary seaman on an English vessel.

In 1884, now using the English name **Joseph Conrad**, he became a master in the English merchant service. Ten years later the effects of a tropical fever forced him to leave the sea. His first novel *Almayer's Folly*, was published in 1895, and the Polish boy who had become a master mariner settled down in Kent to pursue the career of novelist.

His 20 years at sea had a powerful influence on Conrad. Many of the incidents in his fiction had actually happened during his years at sea, thus his task as novelist was largely that of reminiscence. With *An Outcast of the Islands* (1896), *Tales of Unrest* (1898), *Lord Jim* (1900), *Youth* (1902), and *Typhoon* (1903), he placed the seas and islands of the Southwest Pacific on the map of English fiction. *The Mirror of the Sea* (1906) and *A Personal Record* (1912) are books of personal reminiscence.

His short story about the African jungle, "Heart of Darkness" (1902), formed the basis for **Francis Ford Coppola**'s 1979 Vietnam War film, *Apocalypse Now*.

Nostromo (1904), a long novel of intrigue which centers on the exploration of a silver mine in a South American country, is both a tale of adventure and a searching study of economic imperialism. Later novels include *The Secret Agent* (1907), a terrorist plot in a London setting, *Under West-*

Joseph Conrad.

ern Eyes (1911), a story of a Russian revolutionist, and *Chance* (1914), the most intricate example of his favorite technique of a tale within a tale and the first of his novels to attract a large public following. Subsequent works include *Victory* (1915), *The Arrow of Gold* (1919), *The Rescue* (1920), and *The Rover* (1923).

Because Conrad combines exciting events with inner meaning, he has been called a romantic realist. His best short stories were collected in 1942 in *A Conrad Argosy*.

William McFee, in his introduction, singled out *The End of the Tether* as containing all the archetypical Conrad elements, such as freshness of vision, irony, the glamour of the Eastern seas, the rascality of white men gone sour, and the splendor of a human soul overwhelmed by fate.

It is hard to define of a fictional character created in literature that has become more of an immortal popular icon than the amazingly perceptive British detective Mr. **Sherlock Holmes**. Holmes uses virtually impossible-to-discern clues to solve baffling mysteries, much to the amazement of his chronicler and loyal side-kick, Dr. **John Watson**. Portrayed in film by many actors, notably **Basil Rathbone** in the 1940s, and **Jeremy Brett** in the 1980s and 1990s, Holmes lives on in the minds of the public.

Sherlock Holmes was the creation of novelist, historical writer, and spiritualist **Sir Arthur Conan Doyle**. He was born in Edinburgh, studied medicine at the University of Edinburgh and practiced at Southsea from 1882 to 1890. In fact, Doyle himself is the model for Dr. Watson.

After traveling in the Arctic regions and Africa, Doyle devoted himself to writing fiction. In 1887, he published *A Study in Scarlet*, in which he introduced his famous Sherlock Holmes, the detective.

Sir Arthur Conan Doyle was "Dr. Watson."

Holmes, based at least partially on Dr. Joseph Bell, an Edinburgh surgeon under whom Doyle studied medicine, solves crimes by deduction, often remote from the scene itself.

Holmes' methods, Doyle acknowledged, were suggested by the detective stories of **Edgar Allan Poe** (see No. 27). Dr. Watson, Sherlock's slow-witted and frequently bungling assistant, afforded a foil for the sleuth's cleverness. Holmes continued his attack on crime until 1927, in such books as *The Sign of Four* (1890), *The Adventures of Sherlock Holmes* (1892), *The Hound of the Baskervilles* (1902), *The Return of Sherlock Holmes* (1905), and *The Case Book of Sherlock Holmes* (1927).

Among Doyle's other works ranged from historical novels such as *Micah Clarke* (1889) and *The White Company* (1891), to his science fiction classic *The Lost World* (1912). The latter is the story of an expedition to the Amazon in which dinosaurs are discovered still alive on a remote plateau.

Late in life Doyle became interested in the supernatural, and this pursuit was reflected in *A History of Spiritualism* (1926) and several other books.

In the late nineteenth and early twentieth century, American literature distinguished itself from that of England through the use of distinctly American settings and situations, as well as through the use of American colloquial language. Aside from **Samuel Clemens** (see No. 45), few writers exemplified this style better than **William Sydney Porter**, who wrote short stories under the pen name **O. Henry**. Born in Greensboro, NC, he had little schooling but managed to acquire a fair education, including a knowledge of French, German, and Spanish.

He worked as a drug clerk, bookkeeper, draftsman, sheepherder, newspaper writer, bank clerk, and pharmacist. Convicted in Austin, Texas on a charge of embezzlement, he served over three years in the Federal penitentiary at Columbus, Ohio, where he wrote several short stories.

After his release in 1901 his literary productivity was enormous. Porter's first book, *Cabbages and Kings* (1904), was a novel, but he is best known for his many books of satirical short stories, especially *The Four Million* (1906) and *Roads of Destiny* (1909). His short story "The Ransom of Red Chief" is particularly characteristic, and is often reprinted in anthologies for young adults.

Porter was a superb storyteller, and wrote in a breezy, colloquial style, using surprising twists of plot for effect. He was largely responsible for popularizing the "formula" short story. A style which evolved in the pulp fiction magazines that proliferated in the first several decades of the twentieth century until they were, in turn, largely rendered obsolete by television in the 1950s and 1960s. With his fast-paced style, he would probably have found himself at home writing for television situation comedies, although, for the most part, these do not possess the delicious and creative plot twists that make Porter's work such a joy.

William Sydney "O. Henry" Porter.

53. RUDYARD KIPLING
1865-1936

Remembered for being a pioneer in the use of animals as characters in children's fiction, **Rudyard Kipling** was a gifted novelist and poet, born in Bombay, India on December 30, 1865. He was educated in England at the United Service College. His mischievous school days were subsequently utilized by him in his tale of schoolboy life, *Stalky and Co.* (1899), in which tale he figures as "Beetle." In 1882 he went to Lahore, India as subeditor of *The Civil and Military Gazette*, where he remained until 1899. During these years he contributed stories and poems about colonial life in India to *The Allahabad Pioneer.* These were later published in book form as *Departmental Ditties* (1886), *Plain Tales from the Hills* (1888), *Soldiers Three, The Story of the Gadsbys, In Black and White, Under the Deodars, Wee Willie Winkie, The Phantom Rickshaw* (1888-89).

Before returning to England at the close of 1889, he made a tour of China, Japan, and the United States, and it was not long after his return that he published his first long novel, *The Light that Failed* (1891). The next six years were spent partly in England and partly traveling in North and South America, Australia, and New Zealand. None of these places influenced his work as much as India.

During his travels, he met and married Caroline Starr Balestier, with whose brother, Wolcott Balestier, he collaborated in a novel called *The Naulahka* (1893). His other publications during this period were *Life's Handicap* (1891), *Barrack-room Ballads* (1892), *Many Inventions* (1893), *The Jungle Book* (1894), and *The Second Jungle Book* (1895). Shortly after his return to England in 1896, he published a volume of

Rudyard Kipling.

poems, *The Seven Seas*. In 1897 he was specially elected to membership at the Athenaeum Club, and in 1907 he received the **Nobel Prize** for literature.

While *The Jungle Book* is his archetypical work drawn from first-hand experiences in India, Kipling produced many other novels. Among the best known are the adventure stories *Captains Courageous* (1897), and *Kim* (1901), considered his greatest novel. *Puck of Pook's Hill* (1906), *Actions and Reactions* (1909), *Rewards and Fairies* (1910), were more introspective, while *Something of Myself* (1936) tended to be autobiographical.

The series of children's tales known as the *Just-So Stories* are first rate classics and have remained in print continuously since they were first published in 1902.

In the pantheon of Irish literature, few names shine brighter than that of **William Butler Yeats**. Not only was he a poet in his own right, but he was also a folklorist who helped to preserve and revive interest in the Irish literature that predated the centuries of brutal colonial rule.

Yeats was born in Sandymount, a suburb of Dublin, the son of the painter **J.B. "Jack" Yeats**. William Butler Yeats strove to create an intellectual and spiritual attitude for Ireland from a myth of the free, cultivated, aristocratic intelligence which he felt was embodied by the life at Lady Gregory's estate at Coole Park.

A friend of Dowson and Johnson, Yeats was a member of the Rhymers' Club, and began his career in the 1890s with the well-received poem "Innisfree." Yeats was an Irish patriot, a supporter of O'Leary, and, with Lady Gregory, a founder of the Abbey Theatre. He fought uncompromisingly for the artistic freedom of the theater, even against Maud Gonne, to whom he was devoted for years. He became a shrewd and skillful man, and his practical and political experience resulted in a period of occasional and personal verse of a very powerful kind. His poetry was never again without the direct, colloquial force that is evident in "On Those That Hated 'The Playboy of the Western World,'"

Yeats devised a "system," which is set forth in *A Vision*. This ambiguous and highly symbolic account of things was built up slowly out of his wife's visions, his reading in philosophy, and his knowledge of esoteric doctrines. Whatever its intrinsic merits, this system helped him, as he said, "to hold in a single thought reality and justice."

This allowed him, that is, to write both directly and symbolically. Thus the poetry of his final period, whether ostensibly occasional, as in "Among School Children," or meditative, as in "Meditations in Time of Civil War," or symbolic, as in "Byzantium," is at once immediate, colloquial, and profoundly eloquent.

Yeats also played an important role in the Celtic Revival of the early twentieth century, in which classic Irish folk legends — including tales of warrior princesses, mythic kings, leprechauns and clurichauns — were popularized in such a way as to help provide an Irish national identity in advance of Irish freedom, which was finally achieved in 1922. T.S. Eliot called Yeats "the greatest poet of our time." In 1923 he was awarded the **Nobel Prize** in literature.

William Butler Yeats.

55. H.G. WELLS
1866-1946

A British historian known for his work as a science fiction pioneer, **Herbert George Wells** was born in Bromley in Kent, and educated at London University, where he majored in biology.

His first book, *Select Conversations with an Uncle* (1895), was followed by *The Time Machine* (1895), the first of a long line of science fiction books. The tale of a man who invents a machine by which he is able to travel through time at will, *The Time Machine* not only coined a new term, it inspired hundreds, if not thousands, of imitations.

Throughout the twentieth century, time travel proved to be a staple of science fiction books, films and television episodes. Nearly all situations involved in the perplexing physics of time travel that have been used by twentieth century science fiction writers were anticipated by H.G.Wells in 1895.

Notable among his later books in the science fiction genre were *The Invisible Man* (1897) and *The War of the Worlds* (1898), which created something of a national panic when it was adapted for radio by Orson Welles in 1938.

In *The Shape of Things to Come* (1933) Wells attempted to predict the events and conditions of the late twentieth and early twenty-first century. His projections of World War II, which hadn't happened yet, contained some interesting accuracies, but the farther he got in time, the more the work devolved into philosophical rambling. Indeed, many of his works were vehicles for his socialist views and his militant latter-day Darwinism, a belief that the "fittest" survive and rise to the top.

The development of these sociological convictions may be traced in *Anticipations* (1901), *A Modern Utopia* (1905), *The World of William Clissold* (1926), and *The Anatomy of Frustration* (1936).

In his massive historical work, *The Outline of History* (1920), Wells sought to clarify the background of man's progress toward efficiency united with liberty. Companion volumes were *The Science of Life* (with Julian Huxley and G. P. Wells, 1929) and *The Work, Wealth and Happiness of Mankind* (1932). However, his most enduring achievements as a writer were realistic novels of contemporary life.

In *Love and Mr. Lewisham* (1900), *Kipps* (1905), and *The History of Mr. Polly* (1910), he humorously discussed the romantic aspirations of the lower middle class. He continued the fictional presentation of modern problems in *Tono-Bungay* (1909), *Ann Veronica* (1909), and *The Research Magnificent* (1915).

Wells also contributed to the propaganda and social discussion which took place during on both World Wars. In *Mr. Britling Sees It Through* (1916) he pictured the life and ideals of an ordinary English family on the home front. His later books, which blended solist ideas with a touch of science fiction, included *The New World* (1935), *The World Brain* (1938), *You Can't Be Too Careful* (1941), and *Mind at the End of its Tether* (1945).

H.G. Wells.

The author of *The Little House on the Prairie* and other books about life on the plains and the Midwest, **Laura Ingalls** was born in the "Little House in the Big Woods" of Wisconsin on February 7, 1867. Laura lived everything that happened in her books. "It is a long story," she wrote, "filled with sunshine and shadow." Laura did in fact grow up in the "Little House on the Prairie" and her family had the experiences about which she wrote. Her "Little House" books are of a way of living that existed in rural America for more than a century, but which had largely disappeared by the time she died in 1957. Through her work, young readers still experience that important formative period for American culture.

The Ingalls lived for a while on their homestead, later moving to De Smet, South Dakota, where her father did carpentry. Laura's family was a key inspiration. Her blind sister Mary lived at home and was always cheerful and busy with her work, her books, and music. Her sister Carrie worked for *The De Smet News* for a while after finishing high school, and then she married a mine owner and moved to the Black Hills. Her sister Grace married a farmer and lived near De Smet. After her marriage to **Almanzo Wilder**, Laura lived for a while in a little gray house on a tree claim, but in 1894 they and their daughter, Rose, left South Dakota in a covered wagon and moved to Rocky Ridge Farm in the Ozarks of Missouri, where they cleared the land and built a farmhouse. Eventually they had 200 acres of improved land, a herd of cows, good hogs, and "the best laying flock of hens in the country." For many years they did all their own work. For recreation they used to ride horseback or in a buggy. They read and played music and attended church socials.

In 1949 Almanzo died at the age of 92. They had been married for 63 years.

Laura Ingalls Wilder.

For many years prior to the publication of her first book, Laura Ingalls Wilder was a columnist for a magazine called *The Missouri Ruralist*, and between 1919 and 1925, she wrote several articles about farm life for *McCalls* and *The Country Gentleman*. In 1930, she began work on a manuscript entitled *Pioneer Girl*, which failed to interest publishers.

However, she did succeed with *The Little House in the Big Woods*, which was published in 1932, and followed by *Farmer Boy* published in 1933.

Her definitive work, *The Little House on the Prairie*, which told of her family's life in what later became Oklahoma, was published to great acclaim in 1935. In 1937, at age 70, she published *On The Banks of Plum Creek*. *By The Shores of Silver Lake* (1939) became a Newbery Honor Book, as did *The Little Town on the Prairie* (1941).

Several years before her husband's death, he and Laura took a trip back to De Smet for a reunion with old friends and to gather material for her book about the blizzard of 1880-1881, which was published in 1940 as *The Long Winter*.

ROBERT FROST
1874-1963

In 1961, **President John F. Kennedy** named **Robert Lee Frost** as the first **Poet Laureate of the United States**. The title was purely honorary and the post was not created officially until 1985.

Frost was born in San Francisco, son of a New England emigre with roots ancestrally in Maine. Frost first came to New England with his mother as a young boy, and grew up in Lawrence, Massachusetts.

His first published poem, his class ode, gave promise of his future greatness. Robert tried working at many trades, from newspaper vendor to welder, and studied at Dartmouth for three months. He and Eleanor were married in 1895, and his marriage was one great steadying influence in his life. The other was his poems, which he wrote continuously for 20 years, though without making much headway with editors. He lived a meager, hand-to-mouth existence, often ragged, often hungry, in mills and shoe factories.

In 1900 his grandfather, who had helped the family out before, gave Robert a farm but, ironically, one in New Hampshire. On this "hardscrabble" place, near Derry, Robert reaped a fine harvest of themes for future poems but little else.

He was a highly unsuccessful farmer, neglecting his cows and crops for literature. He made a modest living as a schoolteacher between 1905 and 1912, but in that year, at his wife's insistence, Robert sold out for $1,500, and went to England, staking his future on becoming a professional poet.

In a thatched cottage in Beaconsfield, Buckinghamshire, he met several Georgian poets and they introduced him to editors. Frost's first two books, *A Boy's Will* (1913) and *North of Boston* (1914), were a London sensation.

The former included "Stopping by Woods on a Snowy Evening" and "The Road Not Taken," his signature work.

Robert Frost.

Robert Frost returned home in 1915 and found himself famous. From then on, with Eleanor's help, he achieved his goal. Frost founded the institution of "poet in residence" at Michigan, Amherst, and Dartmouth, but he was also a visitor at other colleges, and a teacher at Bread-Loaf School, which he helped to found in 1920.

He won the **Pulitzer Prize** in 1924, 1931, 1937, 1943, and many other awards. In the middle of the twentieth century, Frost was regarded as the greatest American poet since **Walt Whitman** (see No. 36). His works included *Mountain Interval* (1916), *New Hampshire* (1923), *West-Running Brook* (1928), *A Way Out* (1929), *The Lone Striker* (1933), *A Further Range* (1936), *From Snow to Snow* (1936), *The Witness Tree* (1942, Pulitzer Prize), (1945) and *A Masque of Mercy* (1947).

He wrote from the perspective of an introspective New Englander, used to hard work and a challenging natural environment.He always believed in his slow and painstaking way in poetry, and time has proved him right.

Born in Allegheny, Pennsylvania, **Gertrude Stein** was educated at Radcliffe College and Johns Hopkins Medical School.

Lured by the literary vitality of turn-of-the-century Paris, she moved to the French capital in 1903 and remained there, through two World Wars, and the rest of her life. She lived there with her brother, an art collector, and her secretary and companion, **Alice B. Toklas**.

Gertrude Stein became a leader of the American expatriate writers' discussion group that formed after World War I that was known as **"The Lost Generation."**

In this context, her home became the salon and meeting place for sung American writers as **Ernest Hemingway** (see No.77), and **F. Scott Fitzgerald** (see No. 75). She also influenced **James Joyce** (see No. 65) and was a close friend of "modern" artists such as **Pablo Picasso** and members of the surrealist movement.

As an art collector, she supported Picasso and his contemporaries and obtained many important early originals for next to nothing when these people were still unknown.

As a writer, she became famous for her linguistic experiments, regarded by some critics as profound, by others as examples of the "cult of unintelligibility."

By dislocating words from their habitual associations, she sought to restore their original force and meaning. Her punctuation was dictated by the rhythms of speech. Her works include *Three Lives* (written in 1909 and edited in 1945), a volume of poems entitled *Tender Buttons* (1919), the novel *The Making of Americans* (1925), and

Gertrude Stein.

two volumes of art criticism, *Portraits and Prayers* (1934) and *Picasso* (1938).

Stein also wrote two operas, both with music by Virgil Thomson, entitled *Four Saints in Three Acts* (1934) and The *Mother of Us All* (1947). She also wrote *The Autobiography of Alice B. Toklas* (1933) and *Paris, France* (1940), both personal accounts of her life in the turbulent interwar period. She and Ms. Toklas remained in France during the Nazi occupation of 1940-1944, but left Paris. After World War II, Ms. Stein published *Wars I Have Seen*, about life under Nazi occupation.

W. SOMERSET MAUGHAM
1874-1965

The English author and popular playwright **William Somerset Maugham** was born in Paris and studied at King's School in Canterbury and at Heidelberg. To please his family he studied medicine and earned his degree at St. Thomas' Hospital, London, although he never actually practiced.

As he turned to writing, his first novel, *Liza of Lambeth* (1897), sketched his experiences in the slums near St. Thomas', but it and three later novels were unsuccessful, so he turned to writing plays.

The success of *Lady Frederick* (1907) started him on a long career as a writer of cynical, witty, sometimes serious plays about English life and society. *The Circle* (1921), *The Constant Wife*, and *The Letter* (1927) are among the best of these. None approach the level of artistic importance found in *Of Human Bondage* (1915), a semi-autobiographical novel based on the first thirty years of Maugham's life and school experiences, which has become a modern classic.

The popular *Moon and Sixpence* (1919), a novel based on the life of the painter Paul Gauguin, was the first of a series of works to reflect the influence of Maugham's visits to the Far East.

Such titles as *On a Chinese Screen* (1922), *East of Suez* (1922), and *The Painted Veil* (1925) are later works that deal with colonial life "east of Suez" in the last days before Britain's once-impregnable empire started to implode.

In 1930, the novel *Cakes and Ale* aroused controversy because the characters bore a "certain resemblance" to contemporary English authors. His later works included his autobiography, *The Summing Up* (1938), written nearly three decades before his death, as well as the novels *Christmas Holiday* (1940), *The Razor's Edge* (1944), *Then and Now* (1946), and *Catalina* (1948). His short stories include "The Mixture as Before" (1940), "Up at the Villa" (1941), and "Creatures of Circumstance" (1947), and his critical essays were published in 1949 as *A Writer's Notebook*.

W. Somerset Maugham.

Born in Chicago in 1875, **Edgar Rice Burroughs** embarked on several unsuccessful business ventures before he began writing science fiction in 1911. In 1914, he published *Tarzan of the Apes*.

This first novel was a success. It helped launch a series of 26 such works on the adventures of an upper class English boy who grew up among the wild animals of Africa. Nothing could have been farther from Burroughs' own life and experiences as he was growing up in the American Midwest during a period of industrial expansion. He picked both upper class England and the jungles of central Africa because both were "exotic" and remote from the lives of his readers.

Burroughs had created a character that would come to life not only in the pages of Burroughs' books, but in film, comic strip, and radio as well.

The **Tarzan** stories were immediately popular and were translated into more than 50 languages.

The most memorable film adaptation came with a dozen films produced by MGM between 1929 and 1949 starring Olympic gold medal winning swimmer **Johnny Weissmuller**. Television adaptations began in the 1950s and contin-

ued for two decades until the idea of a white man as a noble savage in Africa became unpalatable for the politically correct.

Burroughs' series of novels about life on Mars, such as *The Chessmen of Mars* (1922) and *Synthetic Men of Mars* (1940), were extremely interesting and well-crafted, but they never attained the fame of his Tarzan books. Because of the lack of a character as compelling as Tarzan, they failed to gain popular acclaim.

Edgar Rice Burroughs created Tarzan, one of the most enduring characters from the popular culture of the early twentieth century.

61. JACK LONDON
1876-1916

A native son of the Far West, **John Griffith "Jack" London** was the first great novelist to explore Alaska themes. He was to the Arctic what **Herman Melville** (see No. 37) was to the sea.

Jack London was born in San Francisco and as a boy he worked as a ranch hand in various parts of California and sold papers in Oakland. Dropping out of the University of California, the restless London traveled through the western United States, sailed the seas, and took part in the 1898 Gold Rush in the Klondike region on the border of Alaska and Canada's Yukon Territory.

He began to attract attention as a fiction writer in 1900, when several of his particularly powerful and moving short stories appeared in *The Overland Monthly*.

London became widely popular when his novel of life and death in the Arctic wilderness, *The Call of the Wild*, was published in 1903. London wrote other fictional works, several of which included the naturalistic doctrine of "the survival of the fittest." They were derived not so much from Charles Darwin's Theory of Natural Selection, but from London's own experiences in Alaska and the Yukon. His frank descriptions delighted readers, but urban critics, who could not conceive of an environment where humans were not the dominant carnivore, found them frightening.

Notable among his short story collections were *The Son of the Wolf* (1900) and *Children of the Forest* (1902), and such novels as *The Sea Wolf* (1904), *White Fang* (1906) and *Martin Eden* (1909).

When London became a convert to socialism, he wrote powerful works in support of his views, such as *The Iron Heel* (1908), a novel which forecast a fascist revolution in 1932 (Hitler came to power in 1933), and *The War of the Classes* (1905), a collection of essays.

John Griffith "Jack" London brought the lure of the Yukon alive for his readers.

A German-born Swiss novelist whose themes were colored by Eastern mysticism, **Hermann Hesse**'s works enjoyed waves of popularity in his own lifetime. They were adopted by devotees of the "counter-culture" in the 1967-1971 period, when anything having to do with Far Eastern philosophical concepts, or mysticism was fashionable. Hesse was able to satisfy them on both levels.

Hesse was born in Calw, a village in the Black Forest, and in his youth he traveled extensively, both in Italy and in India, where his father and grandfather were missionaries. His education was divided between Germany and Switzerland. The stay in India was influential because it brought him in contact with Buddhist philosophy.

As a boy he studied in a classical school and in a seminary, and later became a minister. For a time he was a bookseller, but he turned to writing. His first novel, *Peter Camenzind*, which was partly autobiographical, was published in 1904. *Siddhartha*, published in 1922, was more biographical, examining the life, times and philosophical ethos of the Indian prince and founder of Buddhism, **Siddhartha Gautama**, known as the **Buddha** or the "Enlightened One."

In 1912 Hesse settled in Switzerland, becoming a Swiss citizen in 1923 after the first World War. Another theme that emerged in his novels is that of the subjugation of the individual by the tyranny of the masses after the war.

Among his other works are *Gertrude and I* (1915), *Demian* (1923), and *Death and the Lover* (1932). In *Steppenwolf*, first published in 1927, Hesse paints a masterful picture of Harry Haller, a man whose dreams and reality melt together into a single colorful fabric touched with madness and esoteric symbolism.

Hesse's later works, such as *Das Glasperlenspeil (The Glass Bead Game)* (1943) are especially complex and mystical. He was awarded the 1946 **Nobel Prize** for literature.

Were Hermann Hesse's dream-like tales semiautobiographical?

Poet and historian **Carl Sandburg** was born in Galesburg, Ill. His education was haphazard, mixed with chores on outlying farms and work in the prairie town of Galesburg. He served in the Spanish-American War as a volunteer with the 6th Illinois Infantry in Puerto Rico.

After the war he used his mustering-out pay to enter Lombard (now Knox) College, which he attended from 1898 to 1902. Sandburg began newspaper work in Milwaukee, served as secretary to the mayor of Milwaukee, and moved to Chicago in 1912 to work on *The Chicago Daily News*.

His reputation as a great national poet began with verse published in 1914 in *Poetry: A Magazine of Verse* and collected in *Chicago Poems* (1916). In these he affectionately celebrated the Windy City as the "Hog Butcher for the World; City of the Big Shoulders," finding beauty in its crudest aspects, defining its essential moods.

Later, in *Cornhuskers* (1918), *Smoke and Steel* (1920), *Slabs of the Sunburnt West* (1922), *Good Morning, America* (1928), and *The People, Yes* (1936), he looked out on the fabric of American life and working people, singing of hobos, harvesters, and dock wallopers.

He wrote with conviction in his belief in the power of the people to see through dishonest institutions and corrupt politicians; to realize the promise of greatness inherent in America.

He relished the color and music of American speech, recording the language of folk songs in his compilation *The American Songbag* (1927), and using a lusty, vigorous contemporary idiom in his stories for children, *Rootabaga Stories* (1922), *Rootabaga Pigeons* (1923), and *Potato Face* (1930).

Primarily a chronicler of American life through his poetry, Sandburg had also developed an interest in American history. As a historian, he is noted for his realistic

Carl Sandburg.

but reverent multivolume study of the life and times of the sixteenth president. These included *Abraham Lincoln: The Prairie Years* (two volumes, 1926) and *Abraham Lincoln: The War Years* (four volumes, 1939), for which he was awarded the **Pulitzer Prize** for history in 1940. Other works are *The Chicago Race Riots* (1919), *Mary Lincoln, Wife and Widow* (with Paul M. Angle, 1932), *Storm over the Land* (1942), *Home Front Memo* (1945), *Remembrance Rock* (1948), a historical novel, and an autobiography, *Always the Young Strangers* (1953). His Complete Poems were published in 1950, winning the Pulitzer Prize or poetry.

64. VIRGINIA WOOLF
1882-1941

The English novelist and essayist **Virginia Stephen** was born in London, the daughter of Sir Leslie Stephen.

She married the economist **Leonard Woolf** in 1912, and together they founded the Hogarth Press in 1917, publishing books by **Katherine Mansfield**, **T.S. Eliot** (see No. 68), and **E.M. Forster**. Forster was an important influence in Virginia's first novel, *The Voyage Out* (1915).

In her short stories, "Monday or Tuesday" (1921), she experimented with subtle, indirect methods of characterization, but in her her later novels, such as the memorable *Jacob's Room* (1922), *Mrs. Dalloway* (1925), and *To the Lighthouse* (1927), she developed a stream-of-consciousness technique resembling that of **James Joyce** (see No. 65). This style, involving prose that flows as it occurs to the writer rather than being shaped and edited, was also prominent in her other works. These included *The Common Reader* (essays, 1925); *Orlando* (1928), a fantastic novel; *A Room of One's Own* (1929); *The Waves* (1931); *Flush* (1933); *The Life of Elizabeth Barrett Browning's Pet Dog* (1940); *Roger Fry* (biography, 1940); *The Death of the Moth and Other Essays* (1942).

Virginia Woolf's fear that she was becoming insane is said to have contributed to her tragic suicide by drowning in 1941.

Virginia Woolf.

One of the most renowned of Irish authors, **James Joyce** was born in Dublin, where he is still regarded as one of the most favored of favorite sons. There are still popular organized tours that visit his haunts around town. After time spent at University College, Dublin, Joyce actually spent most of his life in Paris, Rome, Trieste, and Switzerland, where he died. His first small volume of lyrics, *Chamber Music*, was published in 1907, and was followed in 1914 by *Dubliners*, a collection of short stories comprising a "series of chapters in the moral history of his community."

Perhaps the archetypical James Joyce novel is *A Portrait of the Artist as a Young Man* (1916), an autobiographical novel. It traces the hero, Stephen Dedalus, through Joyce's own emotional and intellectual growth, to the point where he exiled himself from his country. He then discovered in "silence, exile and cunning," the mode of life or of art whereby his spirit could express itself in "unfettered freedom."

Part of a first draft of this novel, edited and published in 1944 from the manuscript in Harvard College Library under the title *Stephen Hero*, offers a revealing artistic comparison with the final version. The themes are the same: his friends, the life of Dublin, Catholicism and art.

Joyce's play, *Exiles*, was published in 1918, and in Paris in 1922 It was the work on which Joyce had been engaged since 1914. *Ulysses* is a 730-page novel about the events of one day (Thursday, June 16, 1904) in the lives of Stephen Dedalus, Leopold Bloom, his wife Molly, and certain other Dubliners. It combines psychological exploration, especially at the subconscious levels, with experiments in style that in sheer virtuosity are unequaled. Its technical and linguistic innovations deeply influenced contemporary writers. Critics interpreted the book, with its Homeric symbol-

James Joyce.

ism, which intrigued the reading public due to its having been banned for several years in England and the United States for sexual frankness. Ironically, these bans were lifted before those in Ireland itself.

In *Dubliners*, critic David Daiches described Joyce as the artist observing his environment, whereas in *A Portrait of the Artist*, he is the artist rejecting his environment, and in *Ulysses*, he is the artist recreating the world he has rejected.

Joyce spent 17 years on *Finnegan's Wake* (1939), exploring still lower reaches of human dream consciousness and experimenting in language to a point where only a few philologists can follow him. Yet anyone with a sensitive ear can derive great pleasure from listening to the reading aloud of *Finnegan's Wake*.

It should be noted in considering the strange stylistic progress from *Dubliners* to *Finnegan's Wake*, that Joyce had very defective eyesight, and perhaps in consequence, his imagination was auditory rather than visual.

Born in Eastwood, Nottinghamshire, **David Herbert Lawrence** was the son of a coal miner and of a well-educated mother. Her devotion to her sons and their devotion to her furnished Lawrence with the theme of his first important novel, *Sons and Lovers*, which was published in 1913.

In the decades after his death, D.H. Lawrence's insights into family conflicts was called "Freudian." This was because the grisly psychoanalytical theories of Sigmund Freud, which were obsessed with perversions such as incest and molestation, were fashionable during the period. However, Lawrence had not studied Freud at the time that he wrote *Sons and Lovers*. Later, in 1922 and 1923, he wrote *Psychoanalysis and the Unconscious* and *Fantasia of the Unconscious*.

D.H. Lawrence was an intensely personal writer, with a gift for lyrical expression and a distrust of intellectual explanations. His thinking has been described as inconsistent and contradictory. It was implied during his life, and not entirely by his detractors, that his "religion" was a belief in the blood and the flesh as being wiser than the intellect.

In keeping with this theme, D.H. Lawrence sought in his stories and novels to portray the drama of the instincts, especially in love and sex relationships. Among the books that reflected these themes were *The Rainbow* (1915), *Women in Love* (1921) and *Lady Chatterley's Lover* (1928), all of which were considered "naughty," even during the 1920s, for their sexual frankness. This, of course, made them quite popular and earned Lawrence a living that allowed him to travel abroad.

Evincing a dislike for the "spirit-killing machine of industrialism" that was popular among the literary set during the prosperous years before the Great Depression, Lawrence travelled to sunny climes such as Australia, Mexico, Sardinia, and New Mexico to "escape from civilization." While on location, he was able to gather local color for use in such fascinating travel books as *Sea and Sardinia* (1921), *Mornings in Mexico* (1927) and *Etruscan Places*, published posthumously in 1932.

D.H. Lawrence.

The first American novelist to win the **Nobel Prize** for literature (1930), **Sinclair Lewis** was born in Sauk Center, Minnesota, which is generally assumed to be the scene of his first successful novel, *Main Street*. Lewis was educated at Yale University, and then drifted into various types of editorial and writing work. His early novels, *Our Mr. Wrenn* (1914), *The Trail of the Hawk* (1915), and *Free Air* (1919), were relatively undistinguished, as were some of his later ones. With *Main Street* (1920), satirizing the quaintness of small town life, he found his genre. In the novels that followed, Sinclair Lewis showed a keen ear for conversational crudities, a sound sense of the technical problems involved in making a living in the United States, and a fine eye for the details of rooms and buildings that are found in America.

Sinclair Lewis.

Babbitt (1922) put a new word into the English language, a word to describe the typical go-getting salesman. The book also helped to define the direction that Lewis would take in writing about American life. He would focus on ordinary people and their working lives against the economic backdrop of the times.

Arrowsmith (1925), written with the aid of Paul De Kruif, displayed the problems of the research scientist. Although Lewis won the **Pulitzer Prize** for *Arrowsmith* in 1926, he refused to accept it. *Elmer Gantry* (1927) lampooned an unscrupulous clergyman, and was based on facts provided by the Rev. L.M. Birkhead. *Dodsworth* (1929), which showed a mellowing of Lewis' point of view, was the story of a businessman who found himself in an emotional vacuum after his business days were over.

In 1935 Lewis attacked fascism in *It Can't Happen Here*, and three years later denounced the radical younger generation in *The Prodigal Parents*. *Gideon Planish* (1943) satirized educational institutions, but some of the old fire was lacking, and the novel seemed less tightly constructed. *Cass Timberlane* (1945) was in the ramshackle tradition of Lewis' earlier novels. *Ann Vickers* and *Mantrap* were dismissed by some critics as an inconsequential discussion of inconsequential emotional problems. But with *Kingsblood Royal* (1947) Lewis returned to major topics again, this time raging against discrimination against African-Americans. *World So Wide* (1951), published posthumously, follows the Jamesian method of study of Americans against a European background.

In the 1930s, Lewis adapted his ideas for the theater, acting, directing, and dramatizing, but without conspicuous success. When his second marriage, to journalist Dorothy Thompson, ended in divorce, descriptions of the "Talking Woman" appeared in Lewis' novels. Unlike other novelists, such as **Hamlin Garland**, who had written bitterly of the Middle West and left it, Lewis tempered his anger with admiration, and spent much of his time in the Zeniths and Grand Republics he satirized.

Born in St. Louis, Missouri, **Thomas Stearns Eliot** graduated from Harvard in 1910 and did graduate work in linguistics and philosophy at the Sorbonne and at Oxford.

His impressions of the intellectual aridness and "emotional dry rot" of his era were first presented in the symbolist poems of *Prufrock* (1917) and the "Sweeney jingles" of *Poems* (1919), and were most profoundly and enduringly expressed in *The Waste Land* (1922).

He gradually accepted formal tradition as a token of intellectual security. An Anglophile after his years in Oxford circles, he became a British citizen in 1927 and a member of the Church of England in 1928.

His politically critical works, *The Sacred Wood* (1920), *For Lancelot Andrews* (1928), and *After Strange Gods* (1934), were largely devoted to the ethical and literary function of tradition. This theme was further expounded in the poem *Ash Wednesday* (1930), a pageant; *The Rock* (1934); and a modern morality play, *Murder in the Cathedral* (1935). Among T.S. Eliot's other works are *Homage to John Dryden* (1924), *The Family Reunion* (1939), *The Idea of a Christian Society* (1940), *Four Quartets* (1943), and the overly-ambitious *Notes Towards the Definition of Culture* (1948).

Much of his later critical work first appeared in *The Criterion*, a periodical which he founded and edited. T.S. Eliot received the **Nobel Prize** for literature in 1948, and his play, a vignette of upper class society, *The Cocktail Party* won a *London Times* award.

The Cocktail Party was first staged in London in 1949 and traveled to New York in 1950, where it won the Times Award and had a successful run on Broadway.

The American-born Anglophile, T.S. Eliot, became a British citizen in 1920.

Popular for her character development and engaging mystery stories, **Agatha Christie** was born in Torquay, England. As a young girl, her sister introduced her to mysteries through Sherlock Holmes stories written by **Sir Arthur Conan Doyle** (see No. 51). Her interest in writing mysteries was sparked, and she began to write her own stories. The result was *The Mysterious Affair at the Styles* (1920).

She invented her own distinguished detectives. **Hercule Poirot** is an eccentric Belgium detective who solves the mysteries and puzzles presented to him by using his "little gray cells" to make deductions and crack the case. Poirot first appeared in the *Mysterious Affair at Styles*, and was later killed off in *Curtain* (1975). This drew such attention that his death made the front page of *The New York Times*. Christie's other well known sleuth was **Miss Jane Marple**, an elderly widower who, with her watchful eye, solved murders and mysteries in her home town of St. Mary's Mead. She first debuted in 1930 in *Murder at the Vicarage,* and continued her pursuit of solving cases and finding murderers until her final appearance in the novel *Sleeping Murder* (1976), which was published after Christie's death.

On a trip to the Middle East in 1930, Christie met her second husband, archaeologist **Sir Max Mallowan** (1904-1978), and she went with him on his yearly digs in Iraq and Syria. These trips inspired her novels *Murder in Mesopotamia* (1930), *Death on the Nile* (1937), and *Appointment with Death* (1938). *Agatha Christie: An Autobiography* appeared in 1977. Christie's play, *The Mouse Trap* opened at the Ambassador

Agatha Christie.

Theater in London in 1952, and has performed ever since; making it the longest running theatrical production. Her play, *Witness for the Prosecution* (1953) received the New York Drama Critics' Circle Award. **Queen Elizabeth II** appointed her a Dame of the British Empire in 1971. Christie's stories are well known for the vivid characters and the detailed plot twists. She was a very productive and imaginative writer who over a span of 50 years wrote 68 novels, 17 plays, and more than 100 short stories, which have been published in 103 different languages all over the world.

Born in Rockland, Maine, **Edna St. Vincent Millay** graduated from Vassar College in 1917 and went to New York City, where she became involved in popular literary circles. She was married in 1923 to Eugen Jan Boissevain.

Published in 1917, *Renascence and Other Poems* was her first volume of verse. It was critically well-received, being marked by refreshing directness, striking technical ability, and a somewhat flippant treatment of traditional themes. This obtrusive, cynical sophistication became more pronounced in *A Few Figs from Thistles* (1920), and appeared in her later work as a mature pessimism. *The Harp-Weaver and Other Poems* (1923), containing some of her finest sonnets, was awarded the **Pulitzer Prize** for poetry in 1923.

Her later works included *The Buck in the Snow* (1928); *Wine from These Grapes* (1934); *Conversation at Midnight* (1937); *Huntsman, What Quarry?* (1939); and *The Murder of Lidice* which she wrote in 1942, after German forces destroyed the city of Lidice in Czechoslovakia and slaughtered its civilian population.

Even as she was working in poetry, Edna St. Vincent Millay was also writing works for the stage. Among her well known plays are *Aria da Capo* (1921), *The Lamp and the Bell* (1921), and *Two Slatterns and a King* (1921). Her works were well-written and acclaimed by critics as being sophisticated and hard-hitting in their views of American life and society of that era.

The book *Distressing Dialogues*, which was published in 1924, was a collection of prose sketches published by Millay under the pseudonym of Nancy Boyd. Three years later, she contributed the libretto for the Opera *The King's Henchman,* with music written by composer **Deems Taylor**; the composer and critic who is remembered for radio broadcasts of New York Philharmonic performances.

Maine-born New York author Edna St. Vincent Millay was considered to be "cynically sophisticated." She was an important member of the New York literary establishment in the middle twentieth century.

71. PEARL BUCK
1892-1973

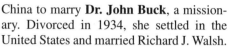

An American novelist whose work focused on the life of rural people in the feudal society of prerevolutionary China, **Pearl Sydenstricker** was born in Hillsboro, West Virginia, but spent her childhood in China with her missionary parents. It was this experience which gave her the background material for her later works of fiction.

She was sent back to the United States to be educated at Randolph-Macon College and Cornell University, but she returned to China to marry **Dr. John Buck**, a missionary. Divorced in 1934, she settled in the United States and married Richard J. Walsh.

Her novels, which are characterized by a deep concern for the human rights of the Chinese peasant, included *East Wind-West Wind* (1930) and *The Good Earth*, her signature work, and that for which she was awarded the Pulitzer Prize in 1932.

She continued this theme with *Sons* (1932), *The Mother* (1934), and *A House Divided* (1935). In 1938, Pearl S. Buck was awarded the **Nobel Prize** for literature.

During World War II, as her beloved China was being viscously mauled by the brutal Japanese Imperial Army, she was active in calling for aid. She played an important part in getting the United States to send humanitarian aid to China during the war, although she was more interested in the human needs of people than in politics.

Her books from that period and in the postwar period, as China sank into first civil war and then Communist tyranny, include *Dragon Seed* (1942), *Yu Lan, Flying Boy of China* (1945), *Pavilion of Women* (1946), *Far and Near* (1947), *The Big Wave* (1947), *Peony* (1948), *Kinfolk* (1949), and *The Child Who Never Grew* (1950).

These books focused on life in China from the perspective of the average Chinese citizens who she knew and loved.

Pearl S. Buck devoted her literary career to acquainting her readers with the everyday reality of life in China.

Dashiell Hammett.

The American detective writer who created **Sam Spade**, the archetypical hard-boiled American private eye, was born in Maryland and educated at Baltimore Polytechnic Institute.

Eight years of experience as a Pinkerton investigator supplied **Dashiell Hammett** with an intimate knowledge of crime detecting and the habits and psychology of criminals. He skillfully exploited this background in a series of detective novels which initiated a realism in the genre that dealt with the seedier side of life.

He was to American detective fiction what **Sir Arthur Conan Doyle** (see No.51) was to British detective fiction. Doyle created **Sherlock Holmes** and Hammett invented Spade. As portrayed on screen by **Humphrey Bogart**, Spade became one of the most copied characters in American film. Countless novels and television series have been produced which feature heroes (and villains) that are the similar to Spade, whose own life was based on Hammett's years as a detective.

Among his best known works are *Red Harvest* (1929), *The Maltese Falcon* (1930), *The Thin Man* (1932), *The Glass Key* (1935) and *Adventures of Sam Spade* (1945). The middle three were all made into films, *The Thin Man* in five films (from 1934 to 1947) starring **William Powell** and **Myrna Loy** and *The Glass Key* in 1942. *The Maltese Falcon* was made three times, in 1931, 1941 and as *Satan Met A Lady* (1936). Directed by **John Huston**, the 1941 film version of *The Maltese Falcon* is regarded as a classic of the first order and is probably the best detective film in the first half century of commercial movie-making. Opposite Bogart as Spade are **Peter Lorre** and **Sydney Greenstreet**, with **Mary Astor** as the cool, corrupt Brigid O'Shaughnessy.

In 1931, Hammett was hired by Paramount to write screenplays, with the most memorable being *City Streets* (1931) and a 1943 adaptation of **Lillian Hellman**'s *Watch on the Rhine*. In 1951 Hammett was jailed for refusing to reveal the source of bail he had helped raise for fugitive communist leaders. He was later charged with tax delinquency by the Internal Revenue Service. After the early 1950s, he never wrote another work.

73. ALDOUS HUXLEY
1894-1963

Born in the village of Godalming, England, **Aldous Huxley** was a member of an illustrious family that included two eminent biologists. His grandfather, **Thomas Henry Huxley**, did field work in the Pacific, and wrote the important textbook *Lessons in Elementary Physiology, Physiography, Anatomy of Vertebrated and Invertebrated Animals*. His brother, **Julian Sorell Huxley**, was both a biologist and a brilliant writer of biological texts and served as chairman of physiology at the Royal Institution.

Aldous Huxley was as brilliant a novelist and author. From 1920, when his witty and popularly disillusioned volume of poetry, *Leda*, appeared, he was critically received as one of the most learned and scintillating "anticipators and reflectors" of many "sophisticated" currents in early to mid-twentieth century fiction, essay, and verse. He began his career in the prosperous years following World War I, when it was fashionable for young men to affect an intellectual negativism. Huxley was no exception, and this characteristic is reflected in such novels as *Crome Yellow* (1921) and *Antic Hay* (1923). Later in the decade, he moved to a more positive humanism with his milestone work, *Point Counter Point*, published in 1928.

In the mid-1940s, the popular trend in English intellectualism and popular literature involved an examination and incorporation of Buddhist philosophy. By then Huxley had become among the most intelligent defenders of what was seen as a return to mystical religion. This was expressed in his best-seller, *Time Must Have a Stop*, published in 1944. The philosophic basis of his shifting position is best revealed in *On the Margin* (1923), *Do What You Will* (1929), *Ends and Means* (1937) and in *Ape and Essence*, published in 1949. Perhaps his best-known work is his wonderful science fiction novel, *Brave New World*, published in 1932, which was glossed over by "serious" historians of literature at the time, but which remains in print today as a monument to his creativity.

Aldous Huxley's account of his own bewildering experiment with LSD, which he described in the popular essay "Doors of Perception," made him something of a minor cult hero in the 1960s. His last work was the utopian *Island*, published in 1962.

Aldous Huxley.

The American author who best typifies the ethos of the flamboyant upper class in the prosperous 1920s, **Francis Scott Key Fitzgerald** was born in St. Paul, Minnesota. He left Princeton to serve in World War I, and it was the university, rather than the war, that would serve as both inspiration and background for his first novel, *This Side of Paradise*. Published in 1920, it reflected the philosophical instability, callow cynicism, and feverish pleasures of postwar adolescents. *The Great Gatsby* (1925), generally regarded as his best book, is the portrait of a bootlegger. It was made into a film in 1974, with **Robert Redford** in the title role. Fitzgerald glamorized Gatsby, for Gatsby lived the life to which Fitzgerald himself aspired.

After 1930, Fitzgerald's work suffered what contemporary critics described as a decline in quality. However, at the time of his death he had begun a promising novel, *The Last Tycoon*. It was to be published posthumously and incomplete in 1941. *All the Sad Young Men* (1926) is representative of several short story collections. *The Crack-Up*, published in 1945, consists of fugitive pieces. The publication in 1950 of *The Disenchanted* by **Budd Schulberg**, a fictional biography of Fitzgerald, and *The Far Side of Paradise* (1951), a real biography by **Arthur Mizener**, reawakened much interest in F. Scott Fitzgerald in the 1950s. Two decades later, the release of the film *The Great Gatsby* helped to create another revival of attention to the works of F. Scott Fitzgerald.

Full of flash and dash, F. Scott Fitzgerald crafted himself in the mold of his character "The Great Gatsby," that is, as the consummate "Roaring Twenties" gentleman.

Ranked with **Ernest Hemingway** and **John Steinbeck** (see Nos. 78, 79) as one of the greatest American novelists of the mid-twentieth century, **William McGraw Faulkner** is also regarded as the definitive Southern writer. He was born in New Albany, Mississippi, but lived principally in nearby Oxford, home of the University of Mississippi.

The prototype of Jefferson in his series of novels centering about the Sartorius family, is identified as his own. The series is concerned primarily with the decadence of Southern character and society in the years following the Civil War.

He was critical of Southern life before the Civil War, but nostalgic for the aristocratic refinements of that lifestyle. This can be seen in such important novels as *Sartorius* (1929), *As I Lay Dying* (1930), *Sanctuary* (1931), *Light in August* (1936), *Absolom, Absolom* (1936), and *The Hamlet* (1940). As a popular short story writer, Faulkner published such collections as *These Thirteen* (1931), *Dr. Martino* (1934), *Go Down, Moses* (1942), and *Knight's Gambit* (1949). His highly complex novel *Requiem for a Nun* (1951) had a complete three-act play in its plot.

Having emerged from obscurity in the South as an author of national and worldwide stature, William Faulkner was elected a member of the American Academy of Arts and Letters in 1948.

He received the academy's Howells Medal for the best United States fiction in the previous five years in 1950. He was awarded the 1949 **Nobel Prize** for litera-

William McGraw Faulkner.

ture, and he received the 1955 Pulitzer Prize for *A Fable* (1954). In 1957, he picked up where he had begun with *The Hamlet* in 1940, publishing *The Town*, a further elaboration of the maternalistic Snopes family. In 1959, he rounded out the Snopes saga as a trilogy with *The Mansion*.

THORNTON WILDER
1897-1975

The definitive American playwright of the middle twentieth century, **Thornton Niven Wilder** was also an important novelist. He was born in Madison, Wisconsin, but he grew up in China, where his father served as an American diplomat. After graduating from Yale in 1920, he studied at the American Academy in Rome. From 1930 to 1936 he lectured on literature at the University of Chicago. Wilder was a complex man, and his understanding of human nature is clearly seen is his character studies.

Thornton Wilder's first novel, *The Cabala* (1926), was followed by *The Bridge of San Luis Rey*, published in 1927, which won him the **Pulitzer Prize** for literature. In this story of eighteenth century Peru, Brother Juniper, a Franciscan monk, traced the lives of five victims of a catastrophe to show that their death was providential.

Heaven's My Destination (1935) was an ironic satire on a contemporary theme, while *The Woman of Andros* (1930) and *The Ides of March* (1948) reflected his interest in classical studies. In his novels involving antique and exotic themes, he displayed a craftsmanship rarely achieved by American writers.

Historians, particularly classically-trained British literary historians, found that Thornton Wilder viewed life narrowly and dispassionately as an ironic miniaturist, and his classicism was relatively contrived.

Nevertheless, audiences responded favorably and his dramatic works were well received and are now regarded as classics. *Our Town* (1938) was a milestone of dramatic fiction, and the rollicking experimental drama, *The Skin of Our Teeth*, earned him the 1942 Pulitzer Prize. Wilder is more often than not regarded as a mature and genuinely inspired reporter on the human comedy.

Among his other important plays were *The Trumpet Shall Sound* (1926), *The Long Christmas Dinner* (1931) and *The Merchant of Yonkers* (1939).

Thornton Wilder collaborated with renowned British filmmaker **Alfred Hitchcock**, producing the screenplay for *Shadow of a Doubt* in 1943. Wilder collaborated on screenplays for *The Bridge of San Luis Rey* and *Our Town*, which was released as a film in 1940. His last and possibly greatest hit was his play *The Matchmaker*, which was published in 1958, and adapted for the stage in 1964 as *Hello Dolly!* Now regarded as one of the greatest and most successful plays ever to appear on Broadway, *Hello Dolly!* was released as a film in 1969.

Thornton Wilder.

One of the twentieth century's greatest authors, **Ernest Miller Hemingway** cultivated an image of author-as-virile-outdoorsman. Born in Oak Park, Illinois, he was educated in public schools and worked briefly as a reporter for a Kansas City newspaper. During World War I he drove an ambulance on the Italian front. Most of his later life was also spent in vigorous, active, often violent pursuits as a soldier, war correspondent, big-game hunter, and deep-sea fisherman. Out of this experience, he developed his primary fiction theme; human beings are most "alive" when acting physically, instinctively and stoically while enduring injury.

Living in Paris after World War I, and influenced by **Gertrude Stein** (see No. 58) and **Ezra Pound**, he polished the terse, economical prose style and clipped making of speech which became widely copied Hemingway trademarks.

Ernest Hemingway.

His first novel, *The Sun Also Rises* (1926), is a story of young, expatriate Americans living in Europe. It was a major work that became a classic of American literature. However, his second, *The Torrents of Spring* (1926), was less well received.

Hemingway's third novel, *A Farewell to Arms* (1929), inspired by his experiences on the Italian front, also a classic work, is a story of love and war. It ranks with **Erich Remarque**'s *All Quiet On The Western Front* as one of the greatest novels of World War I. It was during this early, formative period as a writer that he also produced most of his short stories. Collected in *The Fifth Column and The First Forty-nine Stories*, and published in 1938, they are considered by many as surpassing the quality of even his best novels.

Both *The Fifth Column* and a novel, *For Whom the Bell Tolls* (1940), deal with the struggles of anti-fascists during the Spanish Civil War. From his time spent in Spain, Hemingway wrote *Death in the Afternoon* (1932), a complex discourse on bullfighting.

Big-game hunting in Africa produced the experimental *Green Hills of Africa* (1935), but for the ten years beginning with the start of World War II he wrote little. In 1952, however, his novella, *The Old Man and the Sea*, a story of the acceptance of defeat, was greeted with universal acclaim. *The Old Man and the Sea* also earned Hemingway the 1953 **Pulitzer Prize** for fiction, and in 1954, he was awarded the **Nobel Prize** for literature. His works were well-received because he wrote about rugged individualists, a character type that has always been popular in American fiction.

In the 1950s, he spent much of his time fishing for large game fish in the Caribbean, and as an expatriate in Havana, Cuba. He left after the Castro revolution. His suicide in Idaho in 1961 came as a great shock to his fans and left many unanswered questions about his troubled private life.

Born in Salinas, California and educated at Stanford University, **John Steinbeck** worked as a laborer at various jobs before he took up writing. He published his first book, *Cup of Gold,* in 1929. This was a romantic historical novel about pirate life and the pirate Henry Morgan.

Two other unsuccessful novels followed before *Tortilla Flat* (1935), a novel about Hispanic migrant workers in Monterey County, California won him a wide circle of readers. In *Dubious Battle* (1936) he recounted the story of a strike of migratory workers in California. *Of Mice and Men* (1937) and *The Moon Is Down* (1942) were dramatic novelettes which were successfully translated into plays, and later, films. *Of Mice and Men* was produced as a film in 1940, and *The Moon Is Down* was released in 1943. *Tortilla Flat* was produced by Hollywood in 1942.

John Steinbeck.

The Grapes of Wrath (1939), the story of the fictional **Tom Joad** and his family, was Steinbeck's most popular novel. It was also the one most admired by critics, and in 1940 it was awarded a **Pulitzer Prize**. The Joad family were Oklahoma farmers, known as "Okies," who were driven from the Dust Bowl by extreme poverty and who migrated hopefully to California. Its crusading representation of the social plight of these outcasts led many to compare it with another great fictional work of social comment, *Uncle Tom's Cabin.* The film version of *The Grapes of Wrath* was released in 1940, with **Henry Fonda** in the lead role.

During World War II, Steinbeck also wrote screenplay adaptations of his works *The Lifeboat* (1944) and *A Medal For Benny* (1945).

Steinbeck's other fiction included *Sea of Cortez* (with **E.F. "Doc" Ricketts**, 1941), *Bombs Away* (1942), *Forgotten Village* (1944), *The Wayward Bus* (1947), *The Pearl* (1947), and *Russian Journal* (1948). Through these and his other work, Steinbeck earned a reputation for the accuracy of his dialogue, the naturalism of his characterizations, his sympathetic handling of background, and for the energy and sincerity with which he champions the underdog.

His novel *Cannery Row* (1945) was, like *Tortilla Flat*, set in Monterey County, this time on "Cannery Row," near where he lived. While the sardine industry that supported the canneries later collapsed, the "Row" is a popular tourist destination and Steinbeck's name is invoked in advertising the area more often than he probably would have liked.

His play, *Burning Bright*, was produced in 1950, and he wrote *East of Eden*, which became a classic film starring James Dean (1955), as well as *Wayward Bus* (1967).

GEORGE ORWELL
1903-1950

Born in India in 1903, the son of an English civil servant, **Eric Blair** was educated at Eton, one of Britain's most exclusive schools. He "dropped out" to live a lower class "bohemian" lifestyle, hitchhiking around Europe and the slowly decaying British Empire, working at odd jobs, such as dish-washing. He began his career as a writer under the nom de plume **George Orwell**, and wrote of his early world travels in *Down and Out in Paris and London* (1933) and *Burmese Days* (1934).

In the 1930s, Soviet-style communism held a great fascination for Europe's young, liberal, college-educated elite. When the Soviets threw their support behind the leftist faction in the Spanish Civil War, many young men of the liberal bent. Orwell joined their side and actually went to Spain to fight the German-supported fascist faction. Orwell's great *Homage to Catalonia* (1938) came out of his participation in the Spanish Civil War. Among his other works are *Road to Wigan Pier* (1937), *Coming Up*

for Air (1939), *Critical Essays* (1946), and *The English People* (1947).

After World War II, Orwell's socialism and contempt for totalitarianism was reflected in the clever satire *Animal Farm* (1945). This theme also appeared in *1984* (1949), which predicted the future as it would exist in 1984, when society was ruled by a powerful, but unseen, dictator. This ruler, known simply as "Big Brother," ruled through the use of complex and clandestine surveillance techniques. Orwell picked the title at random by inverting the digits of 1948, the year he wrote it.

Although Orwell's pessimistic vision of 1984 did not actually come to pass, *1984* was extremely popular with the more paranoid of leftist activists in the 1960s, who predicted that the then-current United States government was secretly planning to bring about a society such as Orwell predicted. While *1984* is no longer as popular as it was in the 1960s, *Animal Farm* continues to be a perennial favorite.

George Orwell painted a pessimistic view of the world in 1984.

The 1978 **Nobel Laureate** in Literature, **Isaac Bashevis Singer** was born in Radzymin, Poland, on July 14, 1904, and died in Miami on July 24, 1991. The son and grandson of rabbis, he studied at a rabbinical seminary in Warsaw (1920-1927), before pursuing a career as a writer. He began writing under the influence of his older brother, Israel Joshua, who became a well-known writer himself. After working as a journalist for the Yiddish press in Poland, he published his first novel, *Satan in Goray*, in 1935. In that year, he followed his brother to New York City and began a lifelong career contributing columns, reviews, stories, and essays to the Yiddish newspaper *The Jewish Daily Forward*.

He was fluent in English, yet Singer always wrote in Yiddish, commenting that "I like to write ghost stories and nothing fits a ghost better than a dying language. The deader the language, the more alive the ghost. Ghosts love Yiddish, and as far as I know, they all speak it. I am sure that millions of Yiddish-speaking ghosts will rise from their graves one day, and their first question will be: 'Is there any new book in Yiddish to read?'"

His themes included the life and folklore of the Eastern European Jews, who like himself, had immigrated to America bringing the Yiddish language with them as part of their culture. Among his more than 40 books were *Gimpel the Fool* (1957), *The Magician of Lublin* (1960), *The Spinoza of Market Street* (1961), *Short Friday* (1964), *The Family Moskat* (1965), *In My Father's Court* (1966), *The Seance* (1968), *A Friend of Kafka* (1970), *Enemies: A Love Story* (1972), *A Crown of Feathers* (1973), *Passion* (1975), *Shosha* (1978), *The Manor* (1979), and *Old Love* (1979).

He also wrote *Reaches of Heaven* (1980), *The Penitent* (1983), *Love and Exile: An Autobiographical Trilogy* (1986), *The Death of Methuselah* (1988), and *The King of the Fields* (1988). Singer's *Collected Stories* was a national best-seller in 1969, and he was the recipient of numerous literary awards including the Nobel, two National Book Awards (1970, 1974), the Louis Lamed Prize, the Epstein Award, The Poses Creative Arts Award, the S.Y. Agnon Gold Medal, and the Handel Medallion.

He was a member of the American Academy and Institute of Arts and Letters as well as being a fellow of the Jewish Academy of Arts and Sciences, and the Polish Institute of Arts and Sciences in America. His work appeared in *The New Yorker, Commentary, Esquire, Partisan Review,* and other magazines.

Two works, *Scum* (1991), and *The Certificate* (1992), were published soon after his death, and his third posthumous novel, *Meshugah* was published by Farrar, Straus and Giroux in 1994.

Isaac Bashevis Singer.

The author of a highly regarded group of long novels in which time and a sense of place are extraordinarily important, **James Albert Michener** was born in New York City in 1907. He later studied at or received degrees from the University of Pennsylvania, the University of Virginia, Ohio State University and Harvard University.

He was an editor with the Macmillan Company in 1941, but his fiction career began with the highly regarded *Tales of The South Pacific* (1947), a collection of essays about life and his own experiences in that area during World War II. The book earned him the **Pulitzer Prize** and was adapted as the Broadway musical, and later the film, *South Pacific.* His early works were deeply effected by his experiences with the people and culture of the Pacific and Japan in the years immediately after the war. These included *Return to Paradise,* (1951), *The Voice of Asia* (1951), *The Bridges at Toko Ri* (1953), *Sayonara* (1954), *Rascals in Paradise* (with A. Grove Day 1957), *The Hokusai Sketchbooks* (1958), *Japanese Prints* (1959) and *Hawaii* (1959).

He later turned to American themes with *The Report of the County Chairman* (1961), *Presidential Lottery* (1969), *The Quality of Life* (1970), *Kent State* (1971), *The Drifter* (1971), *Centennial* (1974), *Sports in America* (1976) and *Chesapeake* (1978).

The latter was among his series of sprawling epic novels which included such later works as *The Covenant* (1980), *Space* (1982), *Poland* (1983), *Texas* (1985), *Legacy* (1987), *Journey* (1988), *Alaska* (1988), *Caribbean* (with John Kings 1989), *Six Days in Havana* (1989) and *Mexico* (1992). To gather material for these books, he travelled extensively as he had in the Pacific and Asia for his works in the 1940s and 1950s.

Late in his life, he turned to writing self-searching autobiographical works such as *The Novel* (1991), *The World Was My Home* (1991), and *Literary Reflections: Michener on Michener, Hemingway, Capote and Others* (1993). Michener was the recipient of the US Medal of Freedom and the Golden Badge of the Order of Merit.

James A. Michener.

The author of several series of very popular children's books, **Beverly Cleary** was born in McMinnville, Oregon in 1916. She studied at the University of California and the University of Washington, and worked as a librarian in Yakima, Washington and Oakland, California in the 1930s and early 1940s before she turned to her writing career.

She fell in love with reading as child, and her books generally deal with the experience of growing up as seen through the eyes of the child. Her most endearing and popular continuing character, Ramona Quimby, was introduced in 1951, but has continued to delight and appear fresh to generation after generation of young readers. Ramona, like Beverly Clearly, is an Oregonian, and her experiences with friends and family, are such that children can identify with.

Her early works, many of which are still in print, include *Henry Huggins* (1950), *Ellen Tebbits* (1951), *Henry and Beezus* (1952), *Otis Spofford* (1953), *Henry and Ribsy* (1954) and *Beezus and Ramona* (1955). Her book *Fifteen* (1956) won the Dorothy Canfield Fisher Children's Book Award (1958).

She went on to write *Henry and the Paper Route* (1957), *The Luckiest Girl* (1958), *Jean and Johnny* (1959), *The Real Mole* (1960), *Hullabaloo ABC* (1960), *Two Dog Biscuits* (1961), *Emily's Runaway Imagination* (1961), *Henry and the Clubhouse* (1962), *Sister of the Bride* (1963) and *Ribsy* (1964), which won her a second Dorothy Canfield Fisher Children's Book award in 1961. *The Mouse and the Motorcycle* (1965), deals with the life from the point of view of a rebellious child who happens to be a mouse.

Other titles in the "Ramona" series include *Ramona the Brave* (1975), *Ramona and her Father* (1977), *Ramona and Her Mother* (1979), *Ramona Quimby, Age 8* (1981), *Cutting Up With Ramona!* (1983), *Ramona Forever* (1984), *The Ramona Quimby Diary* (1984), *The Beezus and Ramona Diary* (1986) and *Meet Ramona Quimby* (1989).

Dear Mr. Henshaw (1983) was written in response to requests for a book about a child of divorced parents, and won a Canfield Award as well as a Newbery Medal and was *The New York Times* Notable Book of 1983.

With the exception of her autobiography, *A Girl from Yamhill: A Memoir* (1988), all of Beverly Cleary's work has been children's fiction. Among her more recent books are *Janet's Thingamajigs* (1987), *The Growing Up Feet* (1987), *Muggie Maggie* (1990), *Strider* (1991) and *Petey's Bedtime Story* (1993).

Beverly Cleary.

83. GRACE PALEY
b. 1922

Born in the Bronx, New York, in 1922, **Grace Paley** attended public schools in New York City and studied at Hunter College and New York University. She began writing poetry in college before turning to short story writing. An extraordinary story-teller, she is one of the most successful American writers devoted almost solely to short stories.

She drew her inspiration from the multitude of languages and dialects she heard being spoken in New York City. She has commented about using her own "Bronx tongue" in her work. In terms of style, she also writes with an interest in what she calls "generational things."

A life-long resident of New York City, with most of the time spent in Greenwich Village, she was honored in 1989 by Governor Mario Cuomo, who declared her the first official **New York State Writer**.

Her work has appeared in *The New Yorker* and *The Atlantic Monthly*, among other publications. Her highly acclaimed collections of stories include: *The Little Disturbances of Man* (1959), *Enormous Changes at the Last Minute* (1974), and *Later the Same Day* (1985). She is also the author of two books of poetry and one collection of poems and prose pieces, *Long Walks and Intimate Talks*.

She is a popular lecturer on the craft of writing and has incorporated her feminist perspective in communicating with her audience. Grace Paley has also taught at Columbia University, Sarah Lawrence, Dartmouth, and the City College of New York.

Included among her many awards and honors are the 1994 Jewish Cultural Achievement Awards (given by The National Foundation for Jewish Culture); the Vermont Award for Excellence in the Arts; the REA Award for Short Stories; and the Edith Wharton Award.

Fellow author Susan Sontag commented that "She is that rare kind of writer, a natural with a voice like no one else's: funny, sad, lean, modest, energetic, acute. Like the great modern Russian writers, she demonstrates a possible unity of the art of consciousness and the naturalness of conscience."

Grace Paley.

Kurt Vonnegut, Jr. was born in Indianapolis in 1922 and dropped out of Cornell University in 1942 to join the US Army. As a prisoner of war, he survived the terrible fire-bombing of Dresden, Germany, an experience which he drew upon in his anti-war novel *Slaughterhouse Five* (1969).

He worked as a reporter at *The Chicago City News* before becoming a fiction writer. His first novel was *Player Piano* (1951), and his second, *Sirens of Titan* (1959), a parody of science fiction, earned him great acclaim. In 1968, he published *Welcome to the Monkey House* (1968), a collection of humorous short stories with Vonnegut's signature biting satire. It was *Slaughterhouse Five*, published at the height of the Vietnam War, that turned Vonnegut into a literary superstar. It led to his becoming a celebrity of the anti-war movement and a popular campus lecturer. The best-seller was followed by a series of pessimistic novels about the decline of American cultural values that included *Breakfast of Champions* (1973), *Slapstick, or Lonesome No More* (1976) and, *Jailbird* (1979). These works captured the pulse of the American mood in the Watergate era, but met with mixed reviews.

Vonnegut published a Christmas story with illustrations by Ivan Chermayeff, *Sun Moon Star*, was published in 1980, and his autobiographical collage, *Palm Sunday,* appeared in 1981.

Despite his wit, dark themes dominate his work and a bout with depression led his attempting suicide in 1984.

Vonnegut's later work included *Galapagos* (1985), a tale about the survival of the fittest that takes place over a million years; *Hocus Pocus* (1990), a deeply pessimistic story about the decay of urban life that takes place in the future; and *Timequake* (1994) another wry tale about moral corruption.

Kurt Vonnegut, Jr.

Born at Long Branch, New Jersey in 1923, **Norman Mailer** served with the US military in the South Pacific during World War II. This experience with helped to define his macho image and which permeated his works, although the war itself is not a prevalent subject.

Mailer studied at Harvard University and at the Sorbonne in Paris and exploded onto the literary scene with *The Naked and the Dead* (1948). He followed this best seller with *Barbary Shore* (1951), *The Deer Park* (1955), *Advertisements for Myself* (1959) and *Deaths for the Ladies and Other Disasters* (1962), a collection of poems.

He soon earned a reputation as a literary tough guy in the same mold as **Ernest Hemingway** (see No. 77.) Later in the 1960s, he wrote *The Presidential Papers* (1963), *An American Dream* (1965), *Cannibals and Christians* (1966), *Why are We in Viet Nam?* (1967), *The Bullfight* (1967), *The Armies of the Night* (1968), and *Miami and the Siege of Chicago* (1968) which received the National Book Award for nonfiction (1968). In 1955, Norman Mailer helped to found *The Village Voice*, the original New York City neighborhood newspaper.

In the 1970s, he wrote the such powerful and graphically explicit works as *King of the Hill* (1971), *The Prisoner of Sex* (1971), *Some Honorable Men* (1975), *Genius and Lust* (1976), *A Transit to Narcissus* (1978), and *The Executioner's Song* (1979), which won him the Pulitzer Prize for Fiction in 1980, and which was a nominee of the National Book Critics Circle.

Not all his works have been fiction. He also wrote the text for two important photographically-illustrated books, *Marilyn* (1973) about Marilyn Monroe, and *The Faith of Graffiti* (1974), which was used in the crusade by some art critics to celebrate New York City subway graffiti as an art form.

Norman Mailer.

Mailer also wrote the plays *The Deer Park: A Play* (1967) and *Strawhead* (1985), as well as the screenplay for *The Executioner's Song* (1982), which earned him an Emmy Award nomination for Best Adaptation. He was the author, producer, director and actor in *Wild 90* (1967) and *Maidstone: A Mystery* (1971).

Despite his well-cultivated "outsider" image, Mailer has earned a number of important literary awards, such as the Edward MacDowell Medal, the Gold Medal of the National Arts Club, In the 1980s, Mailer penned *Of a Small and Modest Malignancy, Wicked and Bristling with Dots* (1980), *Of Women and Their Elegance, Pieces and Pontifications* (1982), *Ancient Evenings* (1983) and *Tough Guys Don't Dance* (1984). During the 1990s, Mailer's works included *Harlot's Ghost* (1991) and the cynical *How the Wimp Won the War* (1991).

86. MAURICE SENDAK
b. 1928

Born in Brooklyn, New York on June 10, 1928, **Maurice Sendak** began writing his own stories when he was nine. After school and on weekends he worked for All American Comics, adapting *Mutt and Jeff* newspaper strips for comic books. Although Sendak had done some book illustrations in 1947 and 1950, the book that he considered his "first real children's book," *The Wonderful Farm* by Marcel Ayme, was published in 1951. The next year he became widely known in the children's book field as the illustrator of the enormously successful *A Hole Is to Dig,* written by Ruth Krauss. He went on to both write and illustrate many important and successful children's books.

Where the Wild Things Are (1963) and *In the Night Kitchen* (1970) clearly established his reputation, and from there he went on to write and illustrate such classic books for children as *Outside Over There, The Nutshell Library,* and *Higglety Pigglety Pop,* as well as having illustrated some 80 books by other writers, notably *The Juniper Tree and Other Tales* from the brothers Grimm. Sendak's numerous awards include the

Maurice Sendak.

Caldecott Medal for *Where the Wild Things Are,* the Laura Ingalls Wilder Award, dozens of citations for best and notable books of the year from *The New York Times Book Review* and the American Library Association, and the coveted Hans Christian Andersen Medal. He was the first American illustrator to receive this honor. *The Art of Maurice Sendak,* by Selma G. Lanes, is an illustrated critical biography.

His work has been displayed in one-man shows at the Gallery of Visual Arts and the Pierpont Morgan Library in New York, at Trinity College in Hartford, at the Galerie Daniel Keel in Zurich, and at the Ashmolean Museum in Oxford.

He adapted his books *The Sign on Rosie's Door* and *The Nutshell Library* for *Really Rosie,* an animated film with music by Carole King that was shown on the CBS television network in 1975, and has since become a popular videocassette. An expanded version of *Really Rosie* with a cast of children opened Off-Broadway in October 1980 and ran for a year. In the 1980s, Sendak designed the sets and costumes for a number of productions of opera and ballet, including *The Magic Flute* (Houston Grand Opera); an opera based on *Where the Wild Things Are* (libretto by Sendak, music by Oliver Knussen, Brussels, Glyndebourne and the New York City Opera); *The Love for Three Oranges* (Glyndebourne, the New York City Opera); *The Nutcracker* (Pacific Northwest Ballet); and Leos Janacek's *The Cunning Little Vixen* (the New York City Opera).

In 1984, his illustrated edition of E.T.A. Hoffmann's *The Nutcracker* was a best seller, and the next year he published *The Cunning Little Vixen.* In 1988 his first collection of essays was published, along with *Dear Mili,* a never-before-published tale written by **Wilhelm Grimm** (see No. 20) and illustrated by Maurice Sendak.

87. TOM WOLFE
b. 1931

The popular and eclectic journalist and author known for his witty style on and off the page, and his passion for "vanilla-colored" suits, **Thomas Kennerly "Tom" Wolfe**, was born in Richmond, Virginia in 1931. He studied at Washington and Lee University and earned his PhD in American Studies at Yale in 1957. Wolfe worked as a reporter on *The Springfield* (Massachusetts) *Union* and *The Washington Post*, before going to New York to work on *The New York Herald Tribune* and *The New York World Journal Tribune*. He was an editor at *New York Magazine* from 1968 to 1976 and at *Esquire Magazine* from 1977. It was here that he developed the genre of "New Journalism," which was the adaptation of fiction style in writing non-fiction.

His first book, *The Kandy-Kolored Tangerine-Flake Streamline Baby* (1965), evolved from a series of New Journalism articles about California custom cars. In his second book, *The Electric Kool-Aid Acid Test* (1968) Wolfe reported on the emerging hippie culture in a best-seller that became an icon of the counter culture.

In *The Right Stuff* (1979), Wolfe took his New Journalism style to the American space program, revealing many details about the private lives of the astronauts. The book earned him the American Book Award and the National Book Critics Circle Award.

Among his other notable works of new journalism are *The Pump House Gang* (1968), *Radical Chic and Mau-mauing the Flak Catchers* (1970), *Mauve Gloves and Madmen, Clutter and Vine and Other Stories* (1976), *In Our Time* (1980) and *From Bauhaus to Our House* (1981).

His first work of pure fiction was *The Bonfire of the Vanities* (1987), a brilliant study in contrasts between the various lifestyles found in 1980s New York City.

Films based on Tom Wolfe's books included *The Right Stuff* and *Bonfire of the Vanities*.

Toni Morrison was born **Chloe Anthony Wofford** in Lorraine, Ohio in 1931. As a child, Toni enjoyed learning about black music, storytelling, myth, and folklore. She graduated from Howard University in 1953 with a degree in English.

Morrison said that she was inspired by "things that had never been articulated, painted, or imagined...about black girls, black women. I don't want to redress wrongs. I want to alter the language and rid it of. . . its racism and fill the void with the voice of black women. It is a risky business." The stories she wrote were often about the suffering of the African-American people and the changes that occurred to the human spirit.

In 1955, she earned her masters degree at Cornell and then taught at Texas Southern University. Two years later, she returned to Howard and married architect **Harold Morrison**. In 1956, she became a textbook editor for Random House, and in 1959 she became a senior editor in its trade department. She was also continuing her teaching career at the State University of New York at Purchase (1969-1970), Yale University (1975-1977), and Bard College (1979-1980).

Toni Morrison.

Setting the tone for later works, her first novel, *The Bluest Eye* (1970), was a novel about a young girl who desired unattainable physical beauty. At the end of the decade, she had written *Sula* (1974), a novel about a 20-year friendship between two girls in the 1920s. Her novel *Song of Solomon* (1977) received the National Book Critics Circle Award and appointment to the American Academy and Institute of Arts and Letters.

In 1978, President Jimmy Carter appointed her to the National Council of the Arts. In 1984, she left her job as a publisher to become the humanities chair at the State University of New York at Albany. She remained there until she accepted the Robert Goheen Professorship on the Coun-

cil of the Humanities at Princeton; making her the first black woman writer to hold a named chair at an Ivy League university.

Noted for her portrayal of black people from all walks of life, she has received numerous honors and awards. Her biography was featured in the PBS Series *Writers in America*.

Her other works include *Tar Baby* (1981), which made her the first black American woman to appear on the cover of *Newsweek*. In 1987 she received the **Pulitzer Prize** for *Beloved*, a moving account about the harsh legacy of slavery. She also advocated an end to the stereotyping of black people.

She received the 1993 **Nobel Prize** in literature for her book *Jazz*. Morrison was the first black person and the eighth woman to win the award.

89. PAUL THEROUX
b. 1941

Paul Theroux was born and raised in Massachusetts. One of seven children, he developed an early interest in books and writing. Theroux graduated from the University of Massachusetts and did graduate work at Syracuse University. In 1963 he joined the Peace Corps, serving as a teacher in Malawi, Africa. He was expelled for espionage after becoming involved with opposition politicians. He took a job as a university lecturer in Uganda, but left in 1968 to assume a teaching position at the University of Singapore when Uganda was consumed by political violence.

Theroux's first novel *Waldo* (1966), written while he was in Uganda, was the story of a man trying to create order in his life. Over the next five years he published three more novels, *Fong and the Indians, Girls At Play,* and *Jungle Lovers.* All three are set in Africa, catching vivid, convincing detail of the hapless collision of Western appetites and ideals with the fragile, uncertain, impoverished new world of Africa.

"Paul Theroux," the South African novelist **Nadine Gordimer** has written, "is without peer as the merciless obituarist of colonialism. He knows his way matchlessly about the milieu where no one was ever at home."

Theroux resigned his position at the University of Singapore in 1971 to devote himself entirely to writing. In the years since, his output has been both prodigious and diverse. *Saint Jack (1963)* was set in Singapore and *The Black House (1974)* was a gothic thriller set in England. His most famous novel, *The Mosquito Coast* (1982) was about a young American living in Central America.

Theroux traveled more than almost any other major writer of his generation. His explorations of the remote, rough corners of the world, and of the complex, troubled nations of Africa, Asia, and Central and South America have been reflected both in the brilliantly observed, compelling setting of his fiction and in his celebrated best-selling books of journeys.

Among his widely read travel books are *The Great Railway Bazaar* (1975), the story of his trek across Asia by train; *The Old Patagonian Express* (1979), about rail travel in South America; and the best-selling *Riding the Iron Rooster* (1988), about his train travels in China. For *The Happy Isles of Oceania* (1992), he travelled the Pacific by boat. In 1995, G.P. Putnam's Sons published his *The Pillars of Hercules: A Grand Tour on the Shores of the Mediterranean.*

Paul Theroux.

90. JOYCE CAROL OATES
b. 1938

One of the most prolific American fiction authors of the latter twentieth century, **Joyce Carol Oates** has written more than two dozen novels and many volumes of short stories, poems, essays, and plays. *The New Yorker* has called this "astounding productivity," while *Time* magazine decried her "appalling prolifacy."

She was born near Lockport, New York and educated at Syracuse University and the University of Wisconsin. She grew up in a poor, rural working class family and her early experiences contributed greatly to the dark earthiness of her characters and story lines.

Her first novel, *With Shuddering Fall* (1964), was about a naive young girl who falls in love with a race car driver. It received mixed reviews, but her second novel, *A Garden of Earthly Delights* (1967) was highly acclaimed and earned her a National Book Award Nomination in 1968). With this story of migrant workers and their struggle for survival, she opened a new insight into poverty.

Expensive People (1967), which also won a National Book Award Nomination was a satire on rich suburbanites.

Her novel, *Them* (1969) won the National Book Award for Fiction. A story of a family living in Detroit from the Depression through the 1967 riots, it was based on her own experiences teaching English at the University of Detroit in the 1960s.

Other important Joyce Carol Oates novels have been *Do With Me What You Will* (1973), *The Assassins* (1975), *The Triumph of the Spider Monkey* (1977), *Bellefleur* (1980), *A Sentimental Education* (1981), *Angel of Light* (1981) and *A Bloodsmoor Romance* (1982).

In her masterful *Mysteries of Winterthorn* (1984), she created a reclusive but compelling female writer in the mold of **Emily Dickinson** (see No. 41), who endures the abuse and repression of brutal and insensitive men.

In the mid-1980s, during which time she chose to write some works under the pen name **Rosamond Smith** to blunt criticism of her "appalling prolifacy," Joyce Carol Oates wrote *Solstice* (1985), *Wild Nights* (1985), *Marya* (1986), *You Must Remember This* (1987) (as Rosamond Smith), *The Lives of the Twins* (1987), *American Appetites* (1989) (as Rosamond Smith) *Soul-Mate* (1989), *Because It Is Bitter and Because It Is My Heart* (1990) (as Rosamond Smith), *Nemesis* (1990), *I Lock My Door Upon Myself* (1990) and *The Rise and Life on Earth* (1991).

Black Water (1992), which she wrote as Rosamond Smith, was inspired by the death of Edward Kennedy's friend Mary Jo Kopechne in 1969. More recent novels which invoke a hard-edged view of modern life include *Snake Eyes* (1992), *Foxfire: Confessions of a Girl Gang* (1993), and *What I Lived For* (1994).

Her poetry collections include *Women in Love* (1968), *Expensive People* (1968), *Angel Fire* (1973), *Dreaming America* (1973), *The Fabulous Beast* (1975), *Season of Peril* (1977), *Women Whose Lives are Food, Men Whose Lives are Money: Poems* (1978), *Luxury of Sin* (1983), *The Time Traveler* (1987), (plays) *The Sweet Enemy* (1965), *Sunday Dinner* (1970), *Miracle Play* (1974), *Three Plays* (1980), *Daisy* (1980), *Presque Isle* (1984), *Triumph of the Spider Monkey* (1985), *In Darkest America* (1990), and *I Stand Before You Naked* (1990). Through the feminism and interest in social justice expressed in her poems, she has inspired younger generations of poets and poetry lovers.

Among the essays penned by Joyce Carol Oates are *The Edge of Impossibility* (1971), *The Profane Art* (1984), *On Boxing* (1987) and (*Woman*) *Writer* (1988).

She has received awards from the Guggenheim Foundation, the National Institute of Arts and Letters, and the Lotus Club, and is a member of the American Academy and Institute of Arts and Letters.

For many years her short stories have been included in the annual Best American Short Stories and the O. Henry Prize stories collections, and she has twice been the recipient of the O. Henry Special Award for Continuing Achievement.

Her collection of stories, *Haunted: Tales of the Grotesque,* was published in paperback by Plumel William Abrahams in 1995. Her 25th novel, *Zombie*, published in 1995, is an unflinching and unforgettable exploration of the twisted mind of a serial killer. Her previous novel, *What I Lived For*, was hailed by James Carroll in *The New York Times Book Review* as "An American Inferno."

She received a National Book Award in 1970 for her novel *Them. Because It Is Bitter, Because It Is My Heart* was nominated for a National Book Award in 1990 and *Black Water* was a finalist for the 1992 National Book Critics Circle Award. In 1990, she was awarded the Rea

Award for the Short Story, given to honor a living American writer who has made a significant contribution to the short story as an art form.

In naming Joyce Carol Oates the 1990 winner, the jury for the Rea Award cited: "One of the magical things about Joyce Carol Oates is her ability to constantly reinvent not only the psychological space she inhabits, but herself as well, as part of her immediate, intuitive understanding — turning to fiction what impinges on her life, wherever she chooses to live it."

With over two dozen novels and other works in print, in Joyce Carol Oates is one of the world's most prolific authors. She has been cited for her "ability to constantly reinvent not only the psychological space she inhabits, but herself as well, as part of her immediate, intuitive understanding — turning to fiction what impinges on her life, wherever she chooses to live it."

91. ANNE RICE
b. 1941

The author that created a literary landscape (or nightscape) populated with vampires, **Anne Rice** was born in New Orleans and grew up fascinated with the occult. As a child, she wandered cemeteries and devoured books about haunted houses. As an adult, she was deeply affected by the death of her mother from alcoholism and her daughter from leukemia.

Married to M. Stan Rice since 1961, she lived in San Francisco for 28 years before returning to New Orleans. Her first novel, *Interview with the Vampire* (published in 1976), took shape during the 1960s. It was a huge best-seller, transforming the shy, secretive woman into a global celebrity, and the character of the vampire "Lestat" into a major fictional icon.

Her initial work was followed by two further works that have been characterized as her "vampire trilogy." *The Vampire Lestat* (1985) and *The Queen of the Damned* (1988), probe deeply into the imaginary lives and worlds of Lestat, his family and his ancestors.

Her vampire novels were accompanied by such important historical novels as *The Feast of all Saints* (1980) and *Cry To Heaven* (1982), which also probe the dark side of the human psyche. She wrote under the penname A.N. Roquelaure, because of explicit sexual frankness. She

also wrote *The Claiming of Sleeping Beauty* (1983), *Beauty's Punishment* (1984) and *Beauty's Release: The Continued Erotic Adventures of Sleeping Beauty* (1985).

In recent works such as *The Mummy or Ramses the Damned* (1989), *The Witching Hour* (1990), *Tale of the Body Thief* (1992), *Lasher* (1993) and *Taltos* (1994), she continued to explore the perspective of occult creatures such as mummies and witches from the inside out.

Anne Rice popularized the vampire genre.

Garrison Edward Keillor was born in Anoka, Minnesota and grew up obsessed with reading and fascinated by the story-tellers on the Grand Ole Opry. The two interests both influenced his later success with the creation of Minnesota Public Radio's *A Prairie Home Companion,* a weekly radio program whose structure is Keillor's on-going story about an imaginary Minnesota town.

He not only raised the radio monologue to new levels of critical respectability, he used his stories as the framework for best-selling books.

The witty, slow-talking host writer and storyteller got his start as a literary magazine editor and campus broadcaster at the University of Minnesota and created *A Prairie Home Companion* in 1979.

His first collection of yarns from his monologue was published in 1982 as *Happy To Be Here*. The second, *Lake Wobegon Days,* became a huge best-seller when it was published in 1985.

Where authors such as **Sinclair Lewis** (see No. 67) insulted Midwesterners in satire, Keillor celebrates small town Midwestern life through his satire. His characters, while parodies, are extremely engaging and interesting.

In 1987, Keillor published *Leaving Home*, which dealt with a move to Denmark and hiatus from *A Prairie Home Companion*, which was intended to be permanent, but which was short-lived. A further anthology of tales was *They Are Still Married: Stories and Letters* (1989), and in 1991, he published the novel *WLT: A Radio Romance*, and *The Book of Guys*.

In addition to his books and radio work, Keillor has contributed articles on American life to magazines and newspapers.

Story-teller and "guy," Garrison Keillor spins yarns of life in Lake Wobegon, Minnesota.

93. ERICA JONG
b. 1942

Writer and poet **Erica Jong** was born in New York City in 1942, the daughter of Seymour and Eda Mirsky Mann. She graduated from Barnard College in 1963 and earned a master's degree from Columbia University in 1965.

She was on the faculty of the English Department of the City University of New York (1964-1965, 1969-1970), and of the overseas division of the University of Maryland from 1967 to 1969.

Her first novel, *Fear of Flying* (1973), put her on the literary map as one of the biggest best-sellers and most talked about books of the year.

In Fear of Flying she dealt with issues such as feminism, guilt, creativity and sex through the experiences of her vaguely autobiographical young protagonist Isadora Zelda White Stollerman Wing. Isadora

reappeared in Jong's second novels, *How to Save Your Own Life* (1977). In this book, the character has matured and is seeking a more fulfilling life. In *Parachutes & Kisses* (1984), Isadora is a divorced mother facing the approach of middle age.

Among her other novels, *Fanny: Being the True History of the Adventures of Fanny Hackabout-Jones* (1980) probes Jong's interest in matriarchal religion and the concept of what she calls the mother-goddess. *Serenissima* (1987) is a historical novel set in eighteenth century England in which the heroine is an actress interested in the occult.

Jong is also a poet and has written several works of non-fiction. These include *Megan's Book of Divorce* (1984); her memoir, *The Devil At Large* (1993); and her autobiography, *Fear of Fifty*, which was published in 1994.

Erica Jong.

94. MICHAEL CRICHTON
b. 1942

Best known as the author of *Jurassic Park*, the novel that was adapted as the biggest-selling film in history, John **Michael Crichton** was born in Chicago on October 23, 1942, the son of John Henderson Crichton and Zula Miller Crichton. He graduated summa cum laude from Harvard University in 1964 and earned his medical degree in 1969.

Crichton was a postdoctoral fellow at the Salk Institute in La Jolla, California from 1969 to 1970, and it was during this time that he started trying his hand as a writer of medical thrillers.

His early success as an author, along with a passion for writing allowed him to devote himself to that craft. However, his medical background has proven to be a valuable asset in crafting works with medical elements or medical themes.

Because he was still eyeing a career in medicine, his early work, primarily mystery thrillers, was published under pen names. As John Lange, he published *Odds On* in 1966, and writing under the name Jeffrey Hudson, he published *A Case of Need*, which earned "Mr. Hudson" the 1968 Edgar Award from the Mystery Writers of America.

Michael Crichton's first book under his real name was *The Andromeda Strain* (1969), which became a popular film. *Five Patients* (1970) earned Crichton the Writer of the Year Award from the Association of American Medical Writers in 1970.

His non-medical thriller, *The Great Train Robbery* (1975) won him his second Edgar award from the Mystery Writers of America.

During the 1980s and early 1990s, he wrote many of the books that would become hit movies. Among his books written during this period were *Congo* (1980), *Electronic Life* (1983), *Sphere* (1987), *Travels* (1988), *Jurassic Park* (1990), *Rising Sun* (1992) and *Disclosure* (1994). *Lost World*, the long-awaited sequel to *Jurassic Park*, was published in 1995.

As a screenplay writer and/or director, Crichton played a key role in such films as *Westworld* (1973), *Extreme Close-up* (1973) *Coma* (1977), *The Great Train Robbery* (1978), *Looker* (1981) and *Runaway* (1984). He also directed the films *Pursuit* (1972) and *Physical Evidence* (1989).

Crichton co-wrote the screenplay for the films *Jurassic Park* and *Rising Sun*, both released in 1993 and based on his novels.

Michael Crichton.

Know for his wry humor and brilliant character development, **John Winslow Irving** was born in Exeter, New Hampshire and has used the state as setting for much of his work.

Irving studied at the University of Pittsburgh in 1961 and the University of Vienna in 1963 and 1964 before going on to earn a degree from the University of New Hampshire in 1965 and a master's in fine arts from the University of Iowa in 1967.

Before taking up writing, or shall we say, before he was published, Irving was the assistant wrestling coach at the Phillips Exeter Academy from 1964 to 1965, and later he was an assistant Professor of English at Windham Collage from 1975 to 1978. In 1981, despite being a best-selling author, Irving returned as the assistant wrestling coach at Northfield Mt. Hermon School (1981-1983), at the Fessenden School (1984-1986), and as the head wrestling coach at the Vermont Academy from 1987 to 1989.

His early novels included *Setting Free the Bears* (1969) and *The 158-Pound Marriage* (1974). His his first major success came with *The World According to Garp* (1978), a family saga about an author and his feminist mother.

The Hotel New Hampshire (1981), also a major best-seller, was an epic that followed a family of innkeepers across four generations. *The Cider House Rules* (1985), was set in a Midwestern orphanage.

His later works include *A Prayer For Owen Meany* (1989), and *A Son of the Circus* (1994).

In developing his stories, Irving has noted that he emulated nineteenth century popular fiction. He noted that he followed the nineteenth century practice of creating a character in which the reader will become involved, and then pull the character through a great many trials and tribulations.

John Irving.

SAM SHEPARD
b. 1943

A prolific playwright and author, who is also an Academy Award-nominated actor, **Samuel Shepard Rogers** was born in Ft. Sheridan, Illinois, but grew up on a Ranch in California. He developed an interest in the lifestyles of cowboys and drifters that he used in many of his plays.

While using the American West as the backdrop for much of his work, he has created an imaginary landscape which is influenced by mysticism and the supernatural.

Sam Shepard.

Having graduated from high school in 1960, he moved to New York City, where the Off-Off-Broadway theater scene was just starting and there was plenty of room for creative young playwrights.

His early work included *Cowboys* (1964) and *The Rock Garden* (1964). He received Obie Awards for *Chicago* (1965); *Icarus' Mother;* (1966); *Red Cross* (1966); *Melodrama Play* (1966) *La Turista* (1967); *Forensic and the Navigators* (1967); *Action* (1974) and *Curse of the Starving Class*;(1977, Obie Award 1977); *Buried Child* (1978) earned him the **Pulitzer Prize** in Drama as well as an Obie. This play, along with *Savage Love* (1979) and *True West* (1981), were violent portrayals of American family life told through black humor.

His best-known work is the 1983 play *Fool for Love*, which won an Obie Award. It is a story of love and incest set in the American West.

Continuing to explore the mythic dimensions of Western lore, he published *The Sad Lament of Pecos Bill on the Eve of Killing His Wife* in 1983. He followed this with *A Lie of the Mind* (1985), which won the New York Drama Critic's Circle Award 1986).

More recent works include *States of Shock* (1991) and *Sympatico* (1993).

Sam Shepard has also penned a number of screenplays that pursue his themes of rebellious loners in a violent or hostile world, many of which are based on his plays. Among them are *Me and My Brother* (1967) *Zabriski Point* (1970) and *Renaldo and Clara* (1978)as well as his great *Fool For Love* (1985). In 1983, German director Wim Wenders commissioned him to adapt his 1982 book Motel Chronicles for the screen. The result was the screenplay for *Paris, Texas* (1984), which won the Golden Palm Award at the Cannes Film Festival. It was the story of a reunion of father and son.

Among his non theatrical fiction are *Hawk Moon: A Book of Short Stories, Poems and Monologues* (1981) and *Rolling Thunder Logbook* (1987), as well as *Motel Chronicles*.

His rough, angular face is best recalled, however, from his work as an actor in such films as *Renaldo and Clara* (1978); *Days of Heaven* (1978); *Resurrection* (1980); *Raggedy Man* (1981), *Frances* (1982); and as test pilot Chuck Yeager in *The Right Stuff* (1983), for which he was nominated for the best supporting actor Oscar. In this role, he portrayed a man much like the heroes in his own plays. He went on to play the lead in the film version of his own *Fool For Love* in 1985.

He has also appeared in *Country* (1984);*Crimes of the Heart* (1986); *Steel Magnolias* (1989); *Hot Spot* (1990); *Bright Angel* (1991); *Defenseless* (1991); *Thunderheart* (1992), and *The Pelican Brief* (1993).

Alice Malsenior Walker was born in Eatonton, Georgia, the daughter of a sharecropper. Her life in the rural South gave her the first hand knowledge of social injustice that would later be so influential to her writing. Her book, *The Third Life of Grange Copeland* (1970), dealt with the story of a black tenant farmer who deserted his family and returned after suffering humiliation in the North to kill his wife.

Having graduated from Sarah Lawrence Collage in 1966, she was writer in residence and a teacher of black studies at Jackson State College (1968-1969), Tougaloo College (1970-1971), and a lecturer in literature at both Wellesley and the University of Massachusetts from 1972 to 1973.

In the 1960s, she was active in the support of the Civil Rights movement and she became an outspoken feminist in the 1970s.

Alice Walker was a Bread Loaf Writers' Conference scholar in 1966 and took first place in the American Scholar essay contest (1967) and won the Merrill writing fellowship (1967).

Noted for her strong advocacy of social justice Alice Walker's early work included *Revolutionary Petunias and Other Poems* (1973), which earned a National Book Award nomination and a Lillian Smith Award from the Southern Regional Council and *In Love and Trouble* (1973), a series of stories about black women. Her book *Meridian* (1976) is considered one of the best novels of the Civil Rights struggle and *You Can't Keep A Good Woman Down* (1981) combines that theme with her feminist ideals.

The Color Purple, published in 1982, is a family epic that deals with the theme of the abuse of women as seen through the eyes of Celie, a southern black woman. The novel earned a Pulitzer Prize for Fiction and the American Book Award for 1983, as well as a National Book Critics Circle Award nomination.

Since the early 1980s, Alice Walker's works have included *In Search Of Our Mother's Gardens* (1983); *Horses Make a Landscape Look More Beautiful* (1984); *To Hell With Dying* (1988); *The Temple of My Familiar* (1989); and *Possessing the Secret of Joy* (1992). She contributed to *Double Stitch: Black Women Write About Mothers & Daughters* (1993) and *Everyday Use* (1994).

Alice Walker.

In 1984, **Tom Clancy** was an obscure Maryland insurance broker with a passion for naval history and only a letter to the editor and a brief article on the MX missile to his credit. Decades earlier, he had majored in English at Baltimore's Loyola College and dreamed of writing a novel. It was his passion for military facts and figures and his deep interest in naval history that would give him the necessary background to achieve that dream.

His first novel, *The Hunt for Red October* (1984), is about a Russian submarine captain who defects, along with his sub, to the United States was a best seller. The book reached *The New York Times* best-seller list after President Ronald Reagan pronounced it "the perfect yarn" and "nonputdownable."

Clancy, who originated the literary genre known as the technothriller, established himself as a master at building realistic fictional scenarios by "turning up the volume" on current events and foreign relations. His second novel, *Red Storm Rising,* took on a US-Soviet tension by providing a realistic modern war scenario arising from a conventional Soviet attack on NATO. Subsequent best-sellers included *Patriot Games*, which dealt with terrorism; *Cardinal of the Kremlin*, which focused on spies, secrets and star wars; *Clear And Present Danger,* concerned a war on drugs; and *The Sum of All Fears* centered on post-Cold-War attempts by terrorists to rekindle US-Soviet animosity.

In *Debt of Honor* (1994), Clancy examined the real-world issues of Japanese-American economic competition, the fragility of America's financial system, and the hazards of US military downsizing.

An avid supporter of the US military, Clancy works in an office lined with war games, books on weapons and government produced maps, all tributes to his lifelong fascination with technology and the military. In turn, he uses his books to advocate a strong American military posture.

The success of his books has resulted in his access to a wide variety of sources and information within military and intelligence circles that sets Clancy apart from other writers of military thrillers.

Tom Clancy.

99. STEPHEN KING
b. 1947

The biggest-selling horror writer of all time and one of the best-selling authors of the twentieth century, **Stephen Edwin King** was born in Portland, Maine on September 21, 1947, the son of Donald and Nellie Ruth Pillsbury King. When Stephen was only two, his father deserted the family, and Stephen grew up lonely and hurt. To fill the void left by the loss of his dad, Stephen created imaginary characters and lost himself in their adventures. He also became an avid reader of science fiction.

He graduated from the University of Maine in 1970 and taught English at the Hampden (Maine) Academy from 1971 to 1973. He was also writer in residence at the University of Maine at Orono from 1978 to 1979. all the while, he was attempting to become able to sustain himself financially through his writing.

His major break came with his novel *Carrie,* (1974), a runaway best-seller about a young girl whose psychic powers include telekinesis.

His subsequent works explore witchcraft and various aspects of the occult to both frighten and delight the readers that make each one into a best-seller. Notable among them are, which *Salem's Lot* (1975), *The Shining* (1976), *Firestarter* (1980), *Cujo* (1981), *Different Seasons* (1982), *Christine* (1983), *Pet Semetary* (1983), *Skeleton Crew* (1986), *The Tommyknockers* (1987), *The Dark Half* (1989), *The Stand (uncut)* (1990), *Four Past Midnight* (1990), *The Dark Tower III: the Waste Lands* (1991), *Needful Things* (1991), *Gerald's Game* (1992) and *Dolores Claiborne* (1992). King also created an original screenplay for *Sleepwalkers* (1991).

As an actor, King has appeared in *Knightriders* (1981), *Creepshow* (1982), *Maximum Overdrive* (1986) and *Creepshow II* (1988). He was the creator and writer of the TV miniseries *The Stand* (1994).

Having read horror and science fiction from an early age, King had developed an intuitive sense of what readers enjoy in a good horror novel. He uses abrupt plot twists for shock value and loves to create imaginary worlds where his characters no longer control their environment. In a Stephen King novel, the characters are completely at the mercy of others, whether those "others" are dark supernatural forces, strange monsters, flesh and blood villains or demons from within themselves.

Among his other interests, King occasionally finds time to play guitar in a rock band called the Rock Bottom Remainders, which is composed entirely of fellow authors, including humorist and columnist **Dave Berry** and **Amy Tan** (see No. 100).

Stephen King.

Born in Oakland, California, **Amy Tan** was raised in towns throughout California, including Fresno, Oakland, Hayward, Santa Rosa, Palo Alto, Santa Clara, Sunnyvale and San Jose. Her father, John Tan, died in 1968. Her first published work was "What the Library Means to Me," published in *The Santa Rosa Press Democrat* in 1960, when she was eight.

Her first published fiction story, "End Game" (later called "Rules of the Game"), appeared in 1986.

She earned a degree in English and Linguistics, and a master's degree in Linguistics from San Jose State University.

She worked as a switchboard operator, an A&W carhop, a bartender and pizza maker as well as a Language Development Consultant to programs for developmentally disabled children. Her writing career began as she was working as a copy writer to a medical education newsletter and as a freelance business writer to high-tech companies, where she specialized in telecommunications.

Amy Tan.

Her first novel, *The Joy Luck Club*, appeared in 1989, and was a massive bestseller. By the time she wrote *The Joy Luck Club*, she had experienced a great deal of life and had a thorough literary education, but for the heart and soul of her first novel, she went back to her roots, basing the book on her life with her own extended family.

The Joy Luck Club is a carefully crafted story about several generations of a Chinese-American family in San Francisco. It was nominated for the National Book Award and National Book Critics Circle Award, and was the recipient of the Commonwealth Gold Award and the Bay Area Book Reviewers Award.

Her second novel, *The Kitchen God's Wife,*(1991) was followed by two children's books, *The Moon Lady*, published in 1992, and *The Chinese Siamese Cat* (1994).

When *The Joy Luck Club* was adapted as a major motion picture in 1994, Amy Tan both co-wrote the screenplay and acted as co-producer.

TRIVIA QUIZ

1. What ancient Greek story-teller crafted tales of talking animals that we still use to teach morals to children?
See Number 2.

2. What great Italian poet wrote an epic poem about hell and was later threatened with death by fire?
See Number 6.

3. What English poet and playwright built a theater that was the largest in the world for its day?
See Number 11.

4. What former sailor became the first important American author of adventure stories about the American frontier?
See Number 21.

5. What French author was given an elaborate state funeral in Paris in 1885?
See Number 22.

6. Who was the American author whose first novel became a massive best-seller and a focal point for the abolitionist movement?
See Number 33.

7. What great Russian novelist died a lonely death in a rural train station?
See Number 40.

Who was the Chicago newspaper editor who created "the wonderful world" of Oz?
See Number 49.

8. What nineteenth century French science fiction writer predicted many twentieth century inventions, some of which didn't come into common usage for over 100 years?
See Number 39.

9. Who was named as the unofficial Poet Laureate of the United States by John F. Kennedy?
See Number 57.

10. Who was the American author whose Paris apartment became the meeting place of "The Lost Generation?"
See Number 58.

11. Which Irish-born author spent 17 years on a complex novel about a Dublin funeral?
See Number 65.

12. What American author complained of American "emotional dry rot" and later became a British citizen?
See Number 68.

13. Who are three authors (one American and two British) who created private detectives that became larger-than-life characters of popular culture?
See Numbers 51, 69 and 72.

14. Who was the medical doctor turned medical fiction author who wrote the novel that was made into the biggest-grossing film in history?
See Number 94.

15. Who had his first novel described as "nonputdownable" by an American president?
See Number 98.

16. What American author once worked as a carhop at a California drive-in soda fountain?
See Number 100.

INDEX

INDEX